Praise for *Because of a Teacher*

"You won't find another compilation like this one! In true Couros fashion, *Because of a Teacher* tells the stories that capture your heart. From the first recounting, you're transported to the moment that someone brought out in you qualities you never knew existed. The memories shared by this amazing group of educators will make you laugh out loud, dry a few tears, and smile more than you have in years. This book celebrates YOU and all that you've given to the children you serve. *Because of a Teacher* is a must-read for all educators. You make a difference every day!"

—**LaQuita Outlaw,** EdD, assistant superintendant for elementary curriculum and instruction

"There may be no better time for a feel-good book of inspirational stories for educators. Not only do these stories warm your heart, they help educators reconnect to their why and reflect back on the influential educators in their own lives. George Couros has curated a book of beautiful reminders of the opportunities teachers and principals have every day to make a difference in the lives of their students and colleagues. Whether you are in your first year of teaching or nearing your last, *Because of a Teacher* will remind you why you went into education in the first place and help us all focus on what is really important: the legacy we will leave with the students and staff we are blessed to work with."

—**Allyson Apsey,** principal and author of *The Path to Serendipity*

"*Because of a Teacher* may make you smile knowingly as you read truths that are close to your own. You may relate to the failures or losses that shaped the journey of these educators. But *all* educators will be driven to reflect on their own journeys in terms of the why that brought them to education, their present educational mindset, and how they plan to take action to affect their future. The powerful stories may help you rediscover your reason for being an educator, rededicate yourself to your educational mission, or just make you remember the amazing community of educators that you are part of."

—**Mike Mohammad,** science teacher

"*Because of a Teacher* is an absolute must-read! Filled with inspiring stories by well-known teachers and impactful voices within the education field, this book reminds educators and educational leaders of their value, their worth, and how their efforts—even in small moments—can make such a significant impact within the school setting. The structure of the book, with its embedded guiding questions, lends itself well to professional-learning discussions and book clubs. I would highly recommend this book to any educator I know!"

—**Morgane Michael,** educational consultant and author of *From Burnt Out to Fired Up!*

"Because of a teacher each of us are able to bless the world with our gifts, talents, and love! Reading this amazing book by George with stories from so many others reminded me of why I chose this noble profession over thirty years ago! I wanted to make an impact and have others love teaching and learning because I existed! I am thankful for my former teachers and mentors and for the honor this book bestows upon them! Read this one soon! It is sure to be a best seller!"

—**Salome Thomas-EL,** award-winning principal, speaker, and author

"Every day we have an opportunity to influence the trajectory of the life of a student. *Because of a Teacher* is filled with voices from the field who remind us of the impact we can make with all students, even on our toughest days. If you are looking for an inspiring read to remind you why you went into the profession, this book is it."

—**Jimmy Casas,** educator, author, speaker, and leadership coach

Because of a Teacher

WRITTEN AND CURATED BY GEORGE COUROS

Because

of a

Teacher

*Stories of the Past to Inspire
the Future of Education*

This book is available at special discounts when purchased in quantity for educational purposes or for use as premiums, promotions, or fundraisers. For inquiries and details, contact the publisher at books@impressbooks.org.

Published by IMPress, a division of Dave Burgess Consulting, Inc.
IMPressbooks.org
DaveBurgessConsulting.com
San Diego, CA

Library of Congress Control Number: 2021941532
Paperback ISBN: 978-1-948334-33-4
Ebook ISBN: 978-1-948334-00-6

Cover design by Emily Mahon
Interior design by Liz Schreiter
Editing and production by Reading List Editorial: readinglisteditorial.com

This entire book is meant to be a dedication to the educators of the past, present, and future. Your legacy lives on in so many people in all aspects of the world. You may never truly get the thanks you deserve, but I wanted to at least try by compiling these stories of gratitude and learning to acknowledge and show appreciation for your incredible work.

Thank you.

Contents

Introduction

GEORGE COUROS

*What greater joy can a teacher feel
than to witness a child's success?*
—Michelle L. Graham

Do you believe, as an adult, your childhood teachers are still cheering you on?

I do. In fact, I know it is true. Former teachers have encouraged me years after I left their classrooms.

Yet it often feels like educators aren't getting the same cheers in return. For every message a teacher receives about the impact they made on the life of a former student, there are countless others that go unsent.

But if you think about it, every student that you have enriched and inspired has probably helped and inspired countless others. We can't quantify a teacher's impact on students because it stretches beyond our comprehension. It is truly immeasurable.

Chronic underappreciation for educators is nothing new. But in 2020, the narrative changed. For a moment, when COVID-19 first hit and many schools moved to home-based learning, the world seemed to recognize the enormity of the task that is teaching. In what felt like a matter of minutes, parents and caregivers started sharing on social media how impossibly hard it was to teach their children at home. If they could not handle their own children at home, they couldn't imagine what it would be like to handle twenty-five to forty kids in a classroom.

Soon, though, the negative comments about teachers returned and education was put in a no-win situation.

If kids went back to face-to-face school, parents raised concerns about safety and the spread of COVID-19. If students continued with virtual or hybrid learning, parents said they couldn't help their kids while working their own jobs. Obviously, people were in so many different and unimaginably tough situations, and it felt like a lot of that stress was directed toward education.

No school or educator is infallible. A lot of them experienced growing pains with their pandemic responses. But the majority of them care deeply about kids and work amazingly hard to do what is best for the children and colleagues they serve.

Changing the Narrative

In light of the past year, I wanted to bring a little light to the education world. This is not to say there aren't any problems, but the problems tend to dominate the narrative in so many aspects of our lives. This is true in all fields, not only in the field of education.

In fact, as educators we can be guilty of only acknowledging negative situations with our direct colleagues. Think about it: How many times have you called your IT department with a problem that needs fixing? And how many times have you called IT just to thank them for the internet working all day in your school or classroom? I know I never have, but it is an easy enough call to make.

You only need to look on social media to see how the negative dominates interactions. Any business has a lot of positive interactions in a day, but usually they go viral when a customer has a negative experience. I used to use my social media accounts to complain about delayed or missed flights, but I rarely (if ever) said anything about the 95 percent of flights that didn't run into issues and provided great service. As a principal, I would focus on the idea that I should "praise publicly and complain privately," but as a human being, I tended to do the opposite on social media.

So, at the beginning of 2021, I started a new series on my *Innovator's Mindset* podcast, which I titled, "Three Questions on Educators that Inspire." I asked educators the following questions:

- Who is a teacher who inspired you and why?
- Who is an administrator who inspired you and why?
- What advice would you give yourself as a first-year teacher?

The first two questions had a very distinct purpose. Not only could my guests share a meaningful practice that inspired them as a student or colleague, but they could also give a much needed shout-out to a former teacher, principal, or superintendent. Who better to change the narrative of education in the world than current educators?

Their stories have the potential to help improve current practice. And they can inspire current teachers while honoring the educators who once inspired them.

This is also an opportunity to encourage others to join the world of education. Around the world, there are fewer and fewer people going into teaching each year. They don't yet know the power that comes with being able to change a young person's life by being there, celebrating who they are, and helping them learn and grow. Often the little things a teacher does each day—stuff so small it doesn't seem like a big deal—make all the difference in the world to a child.

How Far Can Our Stories Reach in Our Current World?

To model the Q and A format for my guests, I answered the three questions myself. Although I discussed the administrator who inspired me and the advice I'd give my younger self (I will share those answers in later chapters), I started by discussing a teacher who inspired me as a student. Unfortunately, I broke my own rules and did not limit my answer to one teacher. I was blessed to have teachers who not only cared about me deeply but also inspired a lot of what I do today. To be fair, I could have shared a lot more than three.

I started with my kindergarten teacher, Mrs. Stock, who made me love going to school on day one. Not only was she incredibly kind and caring, but she always made me feel loved for who I am, which is such an important message to receive at any age.

I remember when we were learning to tie our shoes. She first taught us the easier method of using "bunny ears." It was the first time I was able to tie my shoes on my own and I was so excited. After she taught us the more advanced way to tie our shoes, I told her that I wanted to stick with the bunny method. If it worked for me, I could still use that process, she said. To this day, I make bunny ears when tying my shoes—and I think of Mrs. Stock each and every time I do.

After that, I had to talk about my elementary music teacher, Mrs. Penrose. She had extremely high standards for what she expected from her music class and school concerts, and she inspired me to do better. Because of Mrs. Penrose, I loved being onstage, and she sparked a confidence in me that I didn't have when I first entered school.

As I left elementary school to head off to high school, Mrs. Penrose wrote a heartfelt note to me that I still remember to this day. She thanked me for my dedication to music and acting, and predicted that one day, I would be "performing on a stage." Although puberty did a number on my vocal cords and singing ability, I still believed that I would have the opportunity to be onstage because Mrs. Penrose saw it in me.

Eventually, I became a speaker in education and have had the opportunity to speak to hundreds of thousands of people with a confidence that Mrs. Penrose instilled in me from third grade and onward. When I speak and feel I am inspiring a crowd, I know I learned that from an incredible teacher.

I wrapped up by talking about my PE teacher and football coach, Mr. Hobbs. Coach Hobbs came to my high school as a new teacher when I was a senior. He may have had only one or two years of teaching under his belt at the time, but I'm inspired to this day by the things I learned from him.

I was a cocky football player who felt my four years of playing on the team entitled me to the captain position. And because he was a new coach at our school, I had no issue telling him that was what should happen. He smiled and said, "You think so?"

I did, and I told him as much. He said he looked forward to me proving it, which, to be honest, I thought was ridiculous. I had spent four years on the team, and he had been there for twenty-four hours; I was not the one who needed to prove anything. Still, I took his words to heart and worked extremely hard in the first couple of weeks of practice.

When the day came for Coach Hobbs to name captains, he listed the first four with no mention of my name. He then said, "Oh, by the way, we have one more captain." And he said my name.

I was grateful and relieved. He pulled me aside after practice and said, "You earned the opportunity to become a captain because of your leadership in practice, not because you have been here for four years. Don't ever think in your lifetime that you shouldn't have to earn respect from others and that leadership is something you're entitled to."

I listened, and if I am being honest, it went in one ear and out the other at the time. I was just relieved to be named captain. But as I grew older and had different opportunities and disappointments, I remembered the words of Coach Hobbs. They inspire me to this day. Sometimes our best lessons are taught in the present but only embraced in the future.

I shared variations of these stories on my podcast because my former teachers had such an impact on me. The most amazing part was that Coach Hobbs DM'd me on Twitter and thanked me for sharing, while Mrs. Stock and Mrs. Penrose both commented on YouTube.

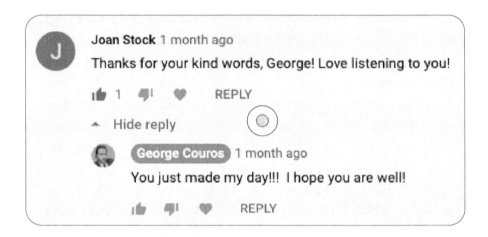

Joan Stock 1 month ago

Thanks for your kind words, George! Love listening to you!

👍 1 👎 ♥   REPLY

▲ Hide reply

George Couros 1 month ago

You just made my day!!! I hope you are well!

👍 👎 ♥   REPLY

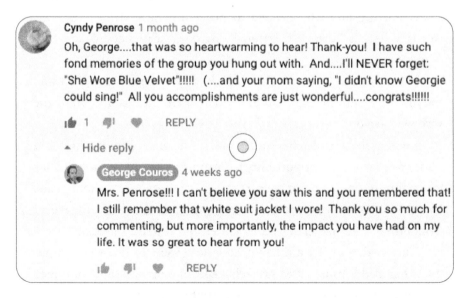

Cyndy Penrose 1 month ago

Oh, George....that was so heartwarming to hear! Thank-you! I have such fond memories of the group you hung out with. And....I'll NEVER forget: "She Wore Blue Velvet"!!!!! (....and your mom saying, "I didn't know Georgie could sing!" All you accomplishments are just wonderful....congrats!!!!!!

👍 1 👎 ♥   REPLY

▲ Hide reply

George Couros 4 weeks ago

Mrs. Penrose!!! I can't believe you saw this and you remembered that! I still remember that white suit jacket I wore! Thank you so much for commenting, but more importantly, the impact you have had on my life. It was so great to hear from you!

👍 👎 ♥   REPLY

I was brought to tears by these teachers' words and the knowledge that they still remembered me.

As I shared at the beginning of this introduction, there are so many teachers who are cheering us on long into adulthood! I am glad that I shared stories about how they molded me as a student and as a person, but I know many more of their students are holding on to similar stories. A compliment shared is never wasted.

What Have We Learned in Our Careers?

These three teachers, and many others I have learned from and/or worked with, have inspired countless students to inspire the world. Yet none of them are perfect and all have grown throughout their careers. This is critical to acknowledge, especially as many new educators come into the profession thinking they will never make that kind of impact.

This is why the third question, "What advice would you give yourself as a first-year teacher?" was so important to ask and answer. I have said countless times that I wish I could go back and apologize to my first-year students because of what I know now. I'm not saying I didn't have an impact on my first class of fourth-grade students. In fact, I still connect with many of those students to this day, and they have shared ways in which I had helped them, which is always great to hear.

If you look back on the beginning of your career and you're not somewhat embarrassed, you might not have grown all that much. Embarrassment over aspects of your early career doesn't mean you were so bad back then; it just points to the fact that you've learned and advanced to get where you are now. Being a learner is paramount to being an educator, and the minute we stop learning is when we should stop teaching. We can't ask others to do what we are unwilling to do ourselves.

Where Are We Going?

As I was answering emails one Saturday afternoon, I read a message from a teacher who was struggling with stress. I thought about my three-question series and how answers from longtime educators could reach those in need of a little encouragement.

This book was born out of my desire to bring together stories from great teachers and administrators. Looking back at what we have learned is much needed "chicken soup" when we are feeling defeated by the stress of education, which never seems to let up. While this book can't ease the complexity of teaching, it can remind you why you went into education and whom you have inspired.

In this book, you will read stories from other educators about the teachers who inspired them, the administrators who believed in them so much they learned to believe in themselves, and the mistakes they have learned from. These stories matter. These ideas from other educators' pasts may inspire you with ideas for the present and the future.

As you read this, I encourage you to think of the teachers and administrators who inspired you, and the advice you would give yourself at the beginning of your career. Share them on social media using the hashtag #BecauseofaTeacher. You may reach an old colleague, reconnect with a teacher who inspired you, and/or inspire the next generation of educators by sharing your story.

But before we move on, I just want to thank you for taking the time to read my story and the stories of others who might not have become educators if it weren't for a teacher. Education is ultimately about changing the trajectory of others in a positive manner. You will never get all of the thank-yous you deserve, but I wanted to at least get you one thank-you closer.

Thank you.

George Couros (aka Mr. Bunny Ears)

MORE ABOUT GEORGE COUROS

George Couros is a worldwide leader in the area of innovative teaching, learning, and leading, and has a focus on innovation as a human endeavor. His belief that meaningful change happens when you first connect to people's hearts is modeled in his writing and speaking. In his  more than twenty years in the field of education, he has worked at all levels of school, including K–12, where he was a teacher, technology facilitator, and school and district administrator. He is currently an adjunct instructor with the Graduate School of Education at the University of Pennsylvania. George is also the author of the book *The Innovator's Mindset: Empower Learning, Unleash Talent, and Lead a Culture of Creativity*. His latest book is *Innovate inside the Box.*

PART I

Who Is a Teacher Who Teacher Who Inspired You and Why?

If You Only Knew

DR. JODY CARRINGTON

Every child deserves a champion—an adult who will never give up on them, who understands the power of connection and insists that they become the best that they can possibly be.
—Rita Pierson

Her name was Mrs. Holly Nordstrom. She taught in a small rural town in a K–12 school that held about five hundred students every year. In 1991, she was my tenth-grade teacher. (She doubled as the school guidance counselor. Like I said, small town.)

Mrs. Nordstrom was a second-generation teacher. Her own children went to this school. The staff room consisted mostly of relatives and at least a few teachers who once attended as students. This farming community was a family. And just like most families, everyone knew everything about everybody. On many days, this wasn't easy.

I started kindergarten with twenty-two other kids. I would attend high school in that same building and graduate with eighteen of those same kids. I can tell you the first and last name of every teacher I had in every one of those grades. I knew where most of them lived. I babysat for a few of them. Made fun of most of them. Admired so many of them.

The school secretary was the same woman throughout my twelve years there—and the mom of the twins in my class. The custodian's name was Mrs. Sheets, and she had the best laugh. My bus driver's name was Stan. He picked me up and dropped me off every day from grades three to twelve. He was a crotchety old soul, and I loved him.

There was something even more special about Mrs. Nordstrom. To this day, I have no idea what class she taught me. It could have been social studies. Or it might have been language arts. I've long forgotten those details, but there's one that has stayed with me all these years.

On April 29, 1991, she delivered one of the most profound lessons I'd ever heard, and it had nothing to do with literacy or numeracy. The day was like any other: teenaged souls trying to navigate friendships and fit in. That sunny afternoon, she gathered us in a small classroom. She stood there, teary, to tell us that one of the kids in our tenth-grade class—a popular, kind, handsome kid named Neil—had been killed that day in an accident during a work experience placement. I remember where she stood as she said those words. I remember what she was wearing. And this sounds creepy even as I write this, but I remember how she smelled (Wild Musk by Coty from the local drugstore). I have no idea what she said, but I vividly remember how I felt. In the midst of a tragedy, as a sixteen-year-old kid, I remember thinking something like this: *if the big people are in charge, the little people will be OK.*

Maybe what I remember most, however, was navigating the next few weeks. I wanted to help somehow and stay connected to his family. I don't remember having conversations about this with my own parents, but I distinctly remember sitting in Mrs. Nordstrom's office and asking her what you do when someone dies. I asked her if I should take things to Neil's parents. She answered all of my questions, so solid and reassuring where I was breaking. I can now imagine that she, too, was heartbroken.

There was no script for this in many of our sixteen-year-old stories. She never stopped saying Neil's name, making it OK for us to keep talking about him, too. As his funeral was planned, she asked his closest friends about the songs he listened to and the things he loved. The first few bars of Garth Brooks's "The Dance" still take my breath away.

I now understand that she was teaching us the difference between grief and mourning. Grief is the response to loss. In fact, where loss lives, grief will follow. Grief is the soul-crushing experience that is, remarkably, universal to us all. Grief pays no mind to age, race, religion, socioeconomic status, or gender identity. It's a unique experience that often occurs in isolation, and it can punch you in the gut when you least expect it.

Mourning, on the other hand, is how you heal. How you make sense of all the pain. Mourning is typically done in connection with others who are also grieving, and it often involves stories, laughter, and joy. Mourning, for school-aged kids trying to figure out how you make sense of loss and grief, often happens at school.

You're not born with the capacity to mourn. Someone has to show you how. For myself and many of my classmates, in the midst of a tragedy full of grief, Mrs. Nordstrom was one of those navigators. Not because she wanted to be or because she had any specific knowledge of how a small community ought to deal with the sudden death of a young man they knew too well. Because she was a teacher. And that's so much of what teachers do. They show students how to make sense of the hard things. Like how to mourn.

As is often the case during transitional moments, I had no idea how much that day and the weeks that followed would affect the way I wanted to show up in the world. Even as I write this, I am fully aware of how much each person in that small school had the potential to (and indeed did) profoundly impact my story.

Now, almost twenty-five years after that day, I am sitting in my office with a PhD. I speak on stages around North America. I have a best-selling book about kids and relationships, another book on the way called *Teachers These Days*, a psychology practice, and a beautiful family. And I am only starting to realize the power of teachers. I have been lucky enough to have had some of the best.

Significant amounts of time and investment are spent on curriculum and programs, training teachers to be pedagogically sound. But none of that mattered that day. And I wonder, truly, if it matters at all in the grand scheme of things. Does it matter during the most important lessons that students learn in any school?

These are lessons of acknowledgment and connection. Lessons that grief will come and that mourning will require bravery. And lessons that we were never meant to navigate any of the hard things alone.

So many of my greatest teachers came in the forms of bus drivers, custodians, and educational assistants. Relationships know no hierarchy, but they know kindness and connection—especially when things are hard. In tough times, you can't tell kids how to manage big emotions; you have to show them. That's where the magic happens. The rest—the integration of literacy and numeracy—will follow accordingly.

Even after telling this story onstage many times, it never occurred to me to tell Mrs. Nordstrom (she will always be Mrs. Nordstrom to me) how important she'd been to me that day. In fact, I didn't do that until I saw her at a talk I gave some twenty years later. She was in the crowd, but as I told the story about how she taught us to make sense of Neil's death, I couldn't look at her. The gratitude, the connection to a woman who felt like home even though I hadn't seen her in over twenty years, sat like a lump in my throat.

I was nervous as I spoke, knowing she was listening. (I never get nervous, by the way.) After the talk, I crossed the school gym to talk to her. I honestly felt like that sixteen-year-old kid again. She had remarried. As she introduced me to her new husband, I asked her if she knew just how amazing she was. Her husband clearly knew, but it appeared Holly, in all her wisdom, had no idea.

I asked her if she remembered that day, addressing a roomful of sixteen-year-olds with news about Neil. She said, and I remember these words distinctly, "Oh, Jody. You never forget losing a student. I loved that boy. But I don't remember talking to you all, specifically, that day."

I assured her that there were nineteen of us who would never forget. And that it changed the trajectory of my life. When I grabbed her hands and thanked her sincerely for all she had given me (and countless other students, no doubt), she responded as most teachers do, "Oh," she said, "it's just what we do."

In my office, I've hung a quote by the philosopher Ram Dass that reminds me of the lesson Mrs. Nordstrom taught me all those years ago. It reads, "We are all here, walking each other home."

It's perhaps the most profound sentence I have ever read. Is there any more important job on the planet? We are all wired for connection—it's biologically necessary, in fact. We have everything we need, in this moment, to do the things that matter most in this world: connect with others, be there for them, and guide them. You, dear teachers, do this every single day. And the vast majority of you have no idea just how many stories you're a part of.

As a mom to school-aged children, I now have a whole new appreciation for teachers who work so hard to hold the emotions of the tiny humans who mean so much to me. The more time I spend talking to educators about trauma, grief, and how relationships are the answer to it all, the better I understand the impact this heart work often has on them. We don't talk about that nearly enough.

And we don't acknowledge just how sacred this work is for so many reasons that have nothing to do with report cards. The best educators who have left the biggest legacies understand one thing: the most important moments in a teacher's career rarely have anything to do with the curriculum. My wish most days is that teachers only knew the scope of their influence. In fact, I think frequent and gentle reminders of the incredible impact you have on so many are critical to keeping your hearts full as you continue to change the world.

In the spirit of all the Mrs. Nordstroms in the world, my hope is that when you get tired, you will think back on the three or four or twenty-five students who you'll never forget. The ones who remembered your birthday. The ones you lost sleep over. The ones you wished you could have back. The ones you considered taking home to raise as your own. The ones who made you question whether you'd survive the school year. The ones who died.

I promise you, if you can picture them in your head right now, they and their families think about you ten times as much. If you only knew. Many of them will never be able to tell you.

As you journey through the stories in these chapters, taking in the ways in which educators have inspired others, I hope you realize how powerful you are. How many stories you're a part of. How many lives you have impacted. I hope you will breathe deeply and know that despite all the heartache, the lost sleep, the lack of support and resources and acknowledgment, you matter more than most in this world. Because you are a teacher. And I, for one, am so grateful you are.

Three Questions for Conversation

1. What are some ways we can recognize our support staff and the contributions they make to our school community?

2. What is one way that we can authentically recognize the contribution of our colleagues as the embodiment of the phrase "We are all here, walking each other home"? At a time when many educators feel underappreciated, how do we ensure that we recognize the excellence in our school community?

3. Think of an experience you had in school that sticks out to you in a positive way. What made that experience special and memorable? How can you recreate that same experience in your own work for the people you serve?

MORE ABOUT DR. JODY CARRINGTON

Dr. Jody Carrington is a renowned psychologist, sought after for her expertise, energy, and approach to helping individuals, teams, and organizations solve their most complex human-centered challenges. A best-selling author and revered speaker, Jody focuses much of her work around reconnection—the key to healthy relationships and productive teams.

Her approach is authentic, real, and often hilarious. She speaks passionately about resilience, mental health, leadership, burnout, grief, trauma, and how reconnection is the answer to so many of the problems we face. Her best-selling book, *Kids These Days,* was published in 2019 and has sold a hundred and fifty thousand copies worldwide. Her second book, *Teachers These Days*, will be released in 2021. Jody's message is as simple as it is complex: we are wired to do the hard things, but we don't have to do them alone; we are so much braver together. You can find out more about Jody's work by following @drjodycarrington on Instagram and Facebook or visiting drjodycarrington.com.

— 2 —

The Art of Relationships

STEVE BOLLAR

*Show up authentically, and synergy
will meet you there.*
—Sanjo Jendayi

Starting at a new school is never easy. But it's a special kind of diffi-cult when you are transferring from a private Christian school to the local public school.

I spent the first four years of my elementary school career as one of the only Black students in class. But that changed in fifth grade, when I walked through the doors of my new public school. Suddenly, just about all of the students were Black.

Yes, I lived in town with everyone else, but my overall experience of attending school was very different. I knew a few people, but not many. And there were *many*. I went from having about fifteen students in my grade to being one of over a hundred students. It was a shock to the system.

Knowing the rules and finding my way wasn't easy. I was looking for something or someone to connect with. That's when I met Mrs. Hammond.

She was the newly hired art teacher. I remember her telling everyone that she may have been new to the school, but she wasn't new to teaching art. Personally, I loved art. I used to draw all the time. So, when it was time for art class, I was head over heels excited to go.

I must admit, at first there was nothing special about the art class or Mrs. Hammond. She was nice enough, sure. And she taught us great projects. But beyond the art, I didn't give her a ton of thought.

After a few months at school, I was still having difficulty fitting in and finding my place. Because of the years I'd spent at the private Christian school, my educational background was culturally different than those around me. I'm not sure how Mrs. Hammond figured it out, but she invited me to come to her art room in the morning before school started, just to hang out. Why in the world would this woman be willing to have me come to her class before school? I was a little bewildered, yet excited for the opportunity.

So, I showed up one morning. And the next and the next. Each time, she asked me how I was doing and let me play music on the radio and draw. She was always extra nice and very supportive, no matter what was happening in my life. She made me feel seen when she stopped what she was doing to look me in the eyes while I spoke.

Over time, I suggested letting a few of my friends hang out in the morning with me. Mrs. Hammond was all for it. By the end of the school year, there was a sizable group of students hanging out in the art room before the school day began. Even though other students were there, Mrs. Hammond made a point to always talk with me and see how I was doing. True, she may not have spoken to me every day. She may have given others as much attention as she did me. Nevertheless, as a young fifth grader navigating the tricky waters of a new school, it meant so much to me.

As I continued through middle school, Mrs. Hammond made a point to stay connected with my family and me. She would call my house and talk with my parents to make sure I was doing well, and over time she developed a positive relationship with my parents. Seriously, who does that?

She wasn't even one of my core subject teachers. But she did talk to them. At times, she would pull me aside to discuss the (good and bad) things she'd heard about me from my other teachers. She saw my art was improving and shared special time to help me get even better. I must admit, the reason why my interest in art grew was because of the attention and support she gave me.

When I reached eighth grade, Mrs. Hammond decided to start an art club. In the process, she asked me what I thought and how it should operate. Sure, she may have talked to other students, but in my eyes, she cared about my opinion specifically. When she asked me to be the very first president of the art club, I nearly passed out. Her acknowledgment of my artistic abilities and my leadership was hugely reassuring and continued to develop me as a leader.

I got another taste of leadership during the school's coveted Be a Staff Member Day. I was chosen to be the art teacher for the day. Talk about a huge honor! I remember trying my best to teach one point perspective to the class and failing miserably. I actually didn't care. It was that moment I fell in love with the idea of becoming an art teacher.

The most exciting part of my middle school experience was when Mrs. Hammond asked me to draw the cover of the yearbook. It was the biggest honor I could think of in my fourteen-year-old life.

Leaving middle school, I was a very different person than the unassuming boy who arrived in fifth grade. Much of my growth as an artist and a person came from the purposeful interest Mrs. Hammond showed me and the connection we forged.

Following eighth-grade graduation, Mrs. Hammond made sure to keep tabs on me. She continued to call my parents to see how I was doing. During the summer, she stopped by my house to take my friends and me to get ice cream. I would visit with her at the middle school and share my artwork with her. She always had time for me.

At the end of my sophomore year in high school, my family moved. We were no longer a part of the same school district. That didn't stop Mrs. Hammond. She made sure to get my new phone number and stay in touch with my parents and me. In the summer, she invited me to her house for lunch and to talk.

During my senior year, I finally decided to go to college to become an art teacher. I was full of such joy and excitement when I let Mrs. Hammond know that I would be following in her footsteps. If it weren't for her, I probably wouldn't have chosen art education. Throughout my time in school, she single-handedly fostered my talent for, interest in, and love of art and teaching.

To be honest, that was just part of my reason for becoming an art teacher. What most inspired me were the connections that Mrs. Hammond had with me and with the other students. As amazing an influence as she was in my life, she inspired others just the same. Not only had she loved her job, but she loved people, too. She cared about how her students grew and the kind of adults they'd become. She took the extra steps necessary to make people feel better. Yes, she had a family, but she treated me and many others as if we were her own children.

Our friendship did not end when I got my high school diploma. Yes, Mrs. Hammond wrote me letters in college. Yes, Mrs. Hammond called my dorm room to see how I was doing and ask about the art projects I was working on. Yes, Mrs. Hammond called my parents to make sure everything was going well.

We had a standing meeting every summer for lunch at her house. She even invited me to bring my girlfriend to meet her. On graduation day, Mrs. Hammond was in the audience to hear me give the graduation speech as class president. She watched me walk across the stage to receive my diploma and later gave me a pair of high-end, professional "art teacher" scissors. (I still have them.)

I was lucky. I was able to obtain a job as an art teacher immediately after graduation. I think Mrs. Hammond was more excited than I was. I remember her calling me after the first week of school to ask how it went, what lessons I taught, and who I connected with.

She insisted that I join the New Jersey Art Educators Association (NJAEA) and shared the importance of connecting with other art educators in order to learn and grow my teaching practice. She even explained how to ensure that the district paid for me to attend so I wouldn't have to pay out of pocket. Of course, I joined. I registered for the conference as early as possible.

On the day of my first conference, I woke up early to drive there, but my beater of a car would not start. I figured that by the time I got it working I would miss the conference. I called Mrs. Hammond and told her that my car didn't work, and I could not make it this year. Immediately, she said she would drive to my apartment and pick me up. Within the hour, Mrs. Hammond was at my front door.

It wasn't until we reached the registration booths that I realized she'd simply come along for my sake. While I hit up the preregistration booth to confirm my arrival, Mrs. Hammond walked over to the on-site registration booth. That's when it hit me: she hadn't registered because she hadn't planned on attending. She attended the conference because of me!

She was there for me that day, just as she'd been there for me most of my life. Even then, long after I'd stopped being her student—after I'd stopped being a student entirely—she took an interest in my well-being and growth.

When I was younger, I had always been appreciative of her guidance and happy to have her around. I'd known that she cared, and I possibly took our relationship for granted at times. But in that moment, when she went to register for the conference, I realized how much Mrs. Hammond loved me. I wasn't just another student who she helped out. To her, I was one of her children, whom she loved dearly. And I loved her. Right after we got our registration tags and bags, I gave her the biggest hug I possibly could, right in front of the registration booth.

Mrs. Hammond was more than an influence in my life. She was able to give meaning and direction. Next to my parents, Mrs. Hammond was the greatest guiding light as I transitioned from childhood to adolescence to young adulthood. She will forever be the reason why I became an educator. From art teacher to principal to superintendent to educational thought leader—I've reached each because she supported me. Thank you, Mrs. Hammond, for being you.

Three Questions for Conversation

1. What are some ways that we can authentically connect with our students to build relationships within our school community? How do we ensure that they know their gifts are valued?
2. What are some of the strategies that you have used in your work to give students ownership of learning, similar to my having the opportunity to be the art teacher for a day?
3. What are some ways that we can develop positive relationships with the caregivers of our students? How will that benefit the learning in our classroom and our overall school community?

MORE ABOUT STEVE BOLLAR

Steve Bollar, aka Stand Tall Steve, is an educational thought leader, former superintendent of schools, principal, author, and a school culture and motivation expert. He is known for his quick wit, creative thought, and humorous personality. This awesome combination and in-depth experience have allowed him to be one of the premier educational/motivational speakers and consultants available. Steve is driven to help schools, associations, and organizations create a better culture and climate through creative innovations and encouragement. His books, *Stand Tall Leadership* and *Ideas, Ideas, Ideas!,* have been a jumping-off place for hundreds of organizations on how to increase morale, change the culture, and improve the climate for their students and staff.

Steve has a long history in the education system, from art teacher to principal to superintendent of schools. His twenty-five-plus-year career has shown him firsthand how to face the challenges that any organization might encounter and how to overcome them with creativity and communication.

It's this insight that he brings to the stage during his keynotes, breakouts, and workshops—training administration, teachers, organizations, and staff how to create a better atmosphere for students and staff alike. You can connect with Steve at @StandTallSteve on Twitter.

— 3 —

Inspiration for a Lifetime and Beyond

DEIDRE ROEMER

The desire to reach for the stars is ambitious.
The desire to reach hearts is wise.
—Maya Angelou

When I started listening to George's new podcast, and to the many stories of inspiring educators, I was flooded with memories of my dad, Bob Driscoll. So, when George asked me the question he poses to all of his guests—Who is a teacher who inspired you and why?—my response was a no-brainer. Of course, I would share my dad's story.

My early memories of my dad are wrapped up in school: in a classroom, in the gym, or with his students and players at our house. I used to love going to work with him, not only to spend time together but also to see the way he interacted with people. The strong connection he had with others was so clearly visible in his conversations. I knew he was something special.

Throughout my childhood, he taught various subjects in a few different schools, but he most loved being an athletic director and coach. I never saw him write a lesson plan or grade a paper, as you would expect to see from most teachers, but I knew he was doing something incredible every day and that he loved his job.

My dad was a storyteller at heart. He knew that a great story could help him connect to students and connect students to content. His stories were animated, elaborate, and highly entertaining with important messages. Admittedly, it sometimes took me a while to figure out the message—it was often tied to lots of statistics and history and usually had a connection to a basketball player or a game. But once I found the message, it was often the exact thing I needed to hear at the time.

His stories engaged and influenced others. They left students laughing. And they have inspired me throughout my life and career. I have used storytelling as a regular part of my teaching and use it now in professional development sessions with staff.

Not only could he tell a great story, but he could also get you to share yours with him. I watched students and players, families and friends, open up to him all the time. He was fiercely empathetic, always paying attention to how others felt or reacted to a situation. He made a point to understand other people's perspectives and often pushed me to do the same.

That is something else I have carried forward. I work hard to know the learners, families, and staff I get to serve now. I want them to feel supported and pushed at the same time. My dad had a remarkable way of doing both, which was a perfect example for me.

We all have a story to tell. Not everyone's stories get to start with, "So, I was talking to Hulk Hogan or Bill Russell . . ." or "I had this big idea, so I'm driving across the country to get to Vegas . . ." But the stories are in each of us. And a whole lot of mine begin with, "This one time my dad and I . . ."

This one time my dad and I took an overnight train from Chicago to Boston. I was twelve, and we were on a father-daughter getaway.

He was always big on grand adventures and making the most of every moment. He didn't let his fear of flying stop us from doing something amazing; he found a way to make it work. We were a middle-class family with a moderate income, but our parents always found ways to give us opportunities to explore the world and do cool things.

When we got to Boston, the first thing we did was go to a Celtics/Lakers playoff game. It was the good old days of Larry Bird, Kevin McHale, Magic Johnson, and Kareem Abdul-Jabbar. We sat a couple of rows behind the bench—a friend of a friend had gotten my dad the tickets and wanted to be sure we had good seats.

Looking back at the experience all these years later makes me realize how lucky my twelve-year-old self was and how I didn't appreciate it as much as I should have. Back then, I soaked up my dad's passion for the sport, but I didn't fully grasp how his connections with people created such a fantastic opportunity for us. How invested he was in spending time together is something I carry with me always.

I often think about using problem-solving skills to open opportunities for myself and others. I think about how the connections we make with others mean something, and how these connections endure. I think about the value of taking the time to get to know someone better and share your passions with them. And I think about risk taking and grand adventures and how their impact lasts a lifetime.

We went on to explore the history of Boston on that trip and then headed to Atlantic City, New Jersey, to check out the boardwalk and the hotels. I can still vividly remember the movement of that train, the sounds of Boston Garden, the taste of the saltwater taffy on the boardwalk, and the love I felt between us. He taught me a great deal in a few short days through a shared experience.

That trip influences how I teach at our local college, how I want our learners to experience school every day, and how I try to support my three children. My husband and I took our children on an overnight train trip from Chicago to Denver a couple of summers ago. We rented a car to drive to all the national parks and went hiking. I can only hope that my own children feel the same influence of that trip as I do from the one I took with my dad when I was twelve.

I wasn't the only person my dad inspired—far from it. Many students and athletes benefited from his ultimate belief in them. He had an incredible capacity to see things in others they did not yet see in themselves.

I remember going to school with him one day and following him to tennis practice. To be honest, I had no idea my dad even knew how to play tennis, much less coach a tennis team. We went from the classroom where I could hear him engaging students with probing questions and big ideas to the tennis court, where he did the same.

He encouraged students with a "You've got this" here and an "I know you can do this" there. He posed a lot of what-if questions: "What if we tried this?" or "What if you thought about it this way?" He used his extraordinary capacity to connect to people to push them to believe in themselves and try anything. He did the same for me throughout my life.

Coaching was such an important part of my dad's life. He spent his summers as a child at Ray Meyer's Basketball Camp in Three Rivers, Wisconsin, learning from Coach Meyer about basketball and life. He got a track scholarship to DePaul University, where Coach Meyer led the DePaul Blue Demons men's basketball team for forty-two years with thirty-seven winning seasons and two trips to the Final Four. True to his connection-forming nature, my dad stayed close with Coach Meyer for the rest of his life. He took many of his players—and my brother and sister—to camp when he became a coach and a teacher.

He truly understood the purpose and intention of coaching team sports. In his view, it was about having a genuine relationship with players and sharing both a common goal and the strategy to achieve it. Getting a group of players to agree on a goal was the easy part. They joined the sport with a goal already in mind: to win and, hopefully, to have fun. But he knew that he could get a group of athletes to agree on an approach to achieving that goal, provided his reasoning was compelling and clear enough that they were willing to take risks to get there. He also knew how important it was for everyone on the team to understand the role they would play in contributing to this unified purpose.

My dad didn't always coach championship teams, but he did create bonds and a sense of purpose, both of which have lived on. His work inspired my siblings and me to coach our own kids. And as an educator, I've always wanted the classrooms in my school to feel the same inspiration and sense of purpose that he coached into every team.

His work inspired my athletic career, too. I played competitive sports throughout elementary school and in my first two years of high school. I enjoyed playing multiple sports, but I did not have the same competitive edge as many other players. Sports were not my passion and my purpose.

They were, however, for my younger sister, whose natural talent was undeniable. She has many other amazing gifts, but what happened when she put a ball in her hands was pretty magical. Knowing she was likely going to play ahead of me on most teams, my dad started to help me find my own purpose.

When I was in middle school, my dad started working a second job in a downtown Chicago restaurant that some of his friends owned. I was interested in that work, so he asked me to join him. On Saturday nights, I headed to my first job, where I'd check diners' coats.

Coat check may seem like a very unusual job for a thirteen-year-old, but it was actually perfect. I would sit in this little booth and do my homework or read while he stood in the lobby and greeted guests. We spent hours each shift talking to each other. He introduced me to famous people who came in for the evening and the not-so-famous people he worked with, some of whom he had known since childhood. We drove thirty minutes to and from the city, and the whole time he told stories of things he saw or his time growing up in Chicago.

By the time I was in high school, he had left teaching and coaching to work in the restaurant business full-time. He moved to a new location, and I went with him most weekends during high school. I graduated from the coat check and moved on to other restaurant roles with more significant responsibilities. By high school, it'd become my full-time summer job, and that continued throughout most of college.

I watched the way he connected with people there the same way I had watched him connect with people in schools. Always the storyteller, he entertained them with tales of his life or the people he'd met. He wanted customers to have the best experience possible when they came to visit. He asked them about their lives, why they chose the restaurant, and how they were enjoying their time at dinner or in the nightclub. He was always looking for ways to improve the experience based on what he had learned about the customers.

At his feet, I learned empathy and how to use the insight I've gained to connect and improve experiences for people. It's a skill I use in my work and my life every day. I know he was not perfect at it, and neither am I, but we both approached the process with the best of intentions and a willingness to try, fail, and try again. Getting it right for others was a huge part of his purpose and has always been a big part of mine.

My dad had a knack for not only spotting talent but also drawing out talent that might need a bit of encouraging. He didn't do this just for student athletes. He helped me develop lifelong skills, as well.

He knew that I had talents off the basketball court that needed to be explored, so he pushed me to do just that. But he didn't just recognize my strengths; he encouraged me in areas of weakness. He knew that my people skills needed some improvement (I was pretty shy at the time) but my organization and problem-solving skills were solid. He found a way to help me grow skills I lacked while shining in areas in which I naturally excelled.

He also found a way to connect with me that was different from how he connected with my brothers and sister. I felt the push to figure out what I wanted to do and how to do it, but I had a lot of support in the process. He pushed risk taking, goal setting, and driving toward our goals with hard work, but he let us set those goals based on our interests and strengths. That is the experience we want to give every learner in every classroom in our schools, and it's how I want my own children to experience life.

My dad also inspired me to see a world outside of my comfort zone. I attended a small parochial school in Wheaton, Illinois, for elementary, middle, and high school. I had the beauty of fantastic learning experiences and incredible teachers throughout my schooling, but almost all of my classmates and teachers shared my background.

Being in downtown Chicago with my dad exposed me to people from many different backgrounds. It opened my eyes to how big the world actually is and how important it is to always surround myself with people who will challenge my thinking and share a different perspective than my own. And, of course, the experience taught me how to engage with others—asking questions and listening to their answers in a genuine effort to connect.

It also taught me that not everyone will want to connect with me, and that's OK. I just need to stay true to myself, be patient when others are not ready to share their story with me, and keep trying. I realized the value of honestly owning a mistake and using it to do better the next time. You'd better believe I took that lesson to heart—and to my classroom.

As educators, we have to keep in mind that it can take multiple tries, with some missteps along the way, to create a relationship with a student. But the time spent is well worth it in the end. The relationships my dad made with players, students, and customers are proof that, at the end of the day, forging connections matters.

Working in restaurants never made me want to become a restaurateur. However, the exposure to the skills I learned in that environment about interacting with people, sharing experiences with them, problem solving, taking risks, and being empathetic have been invaluable to my teaching and my life. My dad was always a teacher and a learner, no matter the setting he found himself in. He encouraged me every day to learn from each interaction and take advantage of every single opportunity I encountered.

Sadly, my dad passed away from pancreatic cancer at the very young age of fifty-two. My older brother, sister, and I were all in college, and my younger brother was seven. It was such a challenging time for us as a family, and for all the people he influenced in his lifetime. He had gone back to coaching a few years before he passed and was starting to get recertified to teach, as well. I am sad that he didn't get a chance to do that before he passed away, and I'm sad that my children, nieces, and nephews never got a chance to meet him. But he lives on in the stories he left behind (we share these often) and the teachers and coaches he left in each one of us.

When my dad passed away, many of his former players and students reached out to our family to share how much of an influence he had on them through sports or the classroom. Several people said things like, "I am the man I am today because of your dad."

I think about that often, not just because it is pretty awesome and a reflection of who my dad really was, but also because it says something about the purpose and intent of school and sports. My dad knew it: the people we serve and the experiences we have together teach us to try new things and help us grow. I feel incredibly fortunate to be the teacher, coach, and mom I am today because of him, too.

Relatives and his old friends regularly tell my siblings and me that he would be so proud of us today. But our achievements are to his credit. And even though he's gone, the lessons he taught me continue to push me to set my sights on any goal, believe in all learners with absolute faith, give them multiple opportunities to try, and be patient until they are ready.

Ironically, as I finished writing this, someone posted an old picture of my dad and a basketball team he coached in 1969. Some of his students from that time started commenting on the image. They shared stories about him opening opportunities for women to play organized sports for the first time. They talked about illnesses and injuries and how he always showed up to offer his support.

They spoke of times he showed his belief in them and connected to them personally to encourage their success. And they spoke of ways he inspired those around him to work hard and bring their best to the task at hand. It was amazing to see that fifty-two years later, so many people had a story to tell about how he affected their lives through his care and leadership.

The power of a caring teacher can be felt for a lifetime.

Three Questions for Conversation

1. How can we use storytelling in our own practice to connect to the work we are doing? What impact does storytelling have on learning in our schools?
2. In classrooms and in our work, it is important that we both "push and support" our learners. We want to challenge them and one another, while letting them know we have their backs. What are some ways we can do this in our work to ensure our students and colleagues feel supported but challenged to grow?
3. People are more likely to "show up" if they feel they are contributing their gifts and strengths to something larger than themselves. In our classrooms and communities, what are some ways we can empower our students and staff to recognize that their contributions matter and that our work is better because of their involvement?

MORE ABOUT DEIDRE ROEMER

Deidre Roemer has served as the director of leadership and learning for the West Allis-West Milwaukee School District for the past five years. Prior to that role, she served for twelve years as the coordinator of special education, an instructional coach, and a classroom teacher for a variety of grade levels in Illinois, Wisconsin, Hawaii, Iowa, and Minnesota. Her educational philosophy has always been to empower every learner with an absolute faith in themselves and to help them to be curious, try anything, work hard, and prepare for life after school. She models creating inclusionary communities when she coaches teachers and leaders and as an adjunct professor at the University of Wisconsin-Milwaukee. You can connect with Deidre on Twitter at @deidre_roemer or follow her blog at leveragepoints.home.blog.

4

Teaching Full Circle

DR. MARY HEMPHILL

*You can't connect the dots looking forward;
you can only connect them looking
backward. So, you have to trust that the
dots will somehow connect in your future.*
—Steve Jobs

My parents and I had walked down this hallway a thousand times. I breathed in the familiar smells coming from the cafeteria as we rounded the corner, waved at my best friend, who stood with her parents in the Media Center, and effortlessly pushed open the heavy brown double doors leading to the primary classrooms.

Three years prior, my mom and dad had held my hands tightly as we walked down the hallway for the first time. It'd been my first day of kindergarten, and I could not contain my excitement. I had been waiting for my first day of school for five whole years, and finally the day had come.

My parents had stopped by the main office to check in and ask for directions. I waited with barely contained excitement, a tight grip on my Cabbage Patch Kids lunch box. After collecting my welcome packet, Mom took my left hand and we started down the hall.

A crisp memory lives in my mind: my dad opening a heavy brown door for my mom and me. At the time, that door seemed like a portal to a world I had yet to discover. And I was absolutely right. I fell in love with school that day—the books, the songs, the teachers, the students! That brown door had opened a world of possibilities for me, and every year at open house I was eager to start a new adventure in learning.

This year, however, as my dad pushed open the brown door, I glanced down the hallway at the primary classrooms. I turned to my mom and said, "Those are the classrooms for babies."

"You're right, Mary," my mom replied. "You are going to the third grade now, and you will be in the upper building!"

With excitement in my eyes, I looked at my dad, who gave me a knowing smile. And for the first time ever, he escorted my mom and me to the big blue door.

The big blue door separated the primary classrooms from the upper elementary school. Walking through that door felt surreal, and I could hardly wait to meet my third-grade teacher, Mrs. Sharon Melvin.

My family and I checked the class list outside the door to ensure that my name was on the roster, and Mrs. Melvin rushed over to welcome us. I will never forget how excited she was to see me. We had never met, but it was almost as if she had been expecting me.

I introduced myself, and Mrs. Melvin wrote my name tag in the most perfect print I had ever seen. While she talked with my parents, I started exploring.

I didn't know it then (I may have been older and wiser, but I was still just a kid) but later I came to realize the importance of what Mrs. Melvin had done. Making students feel welcome in their learning environment is a critical first step for building strong, lasting relationships as an educator. Understanding that students are transitioning from their home environments, where they have established routines, strategies for self-care, and a comfortable communication system allows educators to determine how to develop some of these same components in their classrooms. Although the environment may be different, the need is the same: students seek safety. It's human nature. Mrs. Melvin had created a safe place for amazing learning, growing, and exploring to happen.

Her classroom was different than any I had been in. The attention to detail was uncanny, with each student's textbooks perfectly aligned on the left corner of the desk, a nameplate affixed to the top of each sparkling desk, three perfectly sharpened No. 2 pencils in each desk holder, and a handwritten card from Mrs. Melvin welcoming us to her class. I felt like royalty!

As I slowly examined the classroom, I noted a cozy writing nook complete with kids' floor pillows and bins of pens, pencils, and blank notebooks for each student. There was no time to inspect—my gaze was immediately drawn to the blue, purple, and orange fish in the aquarium near the science corner and the rows of microscopes, goggles, and petri dishes lining the shelves. Every corner of the room was inviting, colorful, and carefully designed with such detail that my new classmates and I could not help but be excited for the first day of school. From the outset, Mrs. Melvin made it clear that we were a family.

Looking back, I'm struck by how adeptly she melded practical skills with the interpersonal. During English Language Arts, she would read a chapter from *Ramona Quimby, Age 8* and teach about main characters and the importance of being honest in the same lesson. Learning our multiplication tables was a lesson on equal number groups and treating others as equals. Time did not stand still in her classroom because we were constantly engaged, constantly learning something new, and constantly having fun along the way.

Mrs. Melvin's classroom was a science lab on Thursdays after lunch, and each of us wore the tiniest white lab jacket and goggles as we examined soil samples and dissected worms. Her classroom was a gymnasium on rainy days, and Mrs. Melvin was the referee for a million rounds of indoor four square.

On Fridays, the excitement in Mrs. Melvin's class rivaled that of a theme park as we watched a newly aired episode of *Reading Rainbow* and spent thirty whole minutes playing one of Mrs. Melvin's Fun Friday board games. There was no better way to end a week of learning, investigating, and growing than going on an adventure with Levar Burton and following it up with Fun Friday games.

Throughout the school year, Mrs. Melvin would make big announcements. She'd call us all to the carpet to let us know our new reading groups, our new lab partners, or perhaps that we would be leading a new mini math lesson. I remember working alongside each of my classmates in some capacity that year. Labels such as "academically and intellectually gifted," "learning disabled," and "behaviorally challenged" faded away in Mrs. Melvin's room. We all had to work together to support one another in our education, and we learned to respect our differences along the way.

Sometimes her announcements were to celebrate our classmates: someone became a big brother, someone learned how to ride a bike, and someone else moved into a new home. Mrs. Melvin supported us through challenging announcements as we grieved the loss of pets, grandparents, and even classmates who had to move away in the middle of the year.

Our fearless leader was consistent and unwavering in her quest to ensure that each of us was treated with fairness and kindness. Each of our voices, our unique personalities, and our struggles had a place in her classroom, and she gave us tools to help navigate each of those experiences. I left Mrs. Melvin's classroom that summer a changed person. I had a deep appreciation for the excitement of learning new things in new ways and an even deeper appreciation for the classmates who were on that journey with me.

Thirteen years later, I stood at the end of the hallway at Southwest Elementary School. I carefully balanced two brown boxes on my knee as I opened that heavy brown door once again.

Walking down that hallway, I glanced to the left, remembering a five-year-old Mary who walked with her lunch box in hand for her first day of kindergarten. The ringing of my phone pierced my thoughts. I placed the boxes on the floor and quickly answered it.

"Hey, Mom!" I said with excitement. "Yes, ma'am. I am here and have almost everything moved in. I cannot wait for you to come see it. As soon as I have everything set up, I'll give you a call to come over. I love you, Mom. Tell Dad I said hello."

I tucked the phone back in my pocket, picked up the brown boxes, and made my way to the big blue door. I walked down that familiar hallway until I spotted an unfamiliar nameplate outside a familiar classroom. It read Ms. Hemphill–Third Grade.

It seemed surreal to be the newest faculty member at Southwest Elementary School, and even more so that I had the honor of teaching in the same classroom that Mrs. Melvin had taught in for thirty-eight years. I placed the boxes on the table near the door and walked over to the bookshelves.

A month prior, Mrs. Melvin had announced her retirement from education, and I was able to visit with her immediately after my college graduation. She hugged me in front of that same bookshelf and told me how proud she was that I had decided to go into teaching. She also revealed that her husband had refused to share his man cave in the garage with almost forty years' worth of educational materials, resources, and books. So, she left her legacy to me. (We had a good cry about that.)

I picked up a literacy workbook and ran my hand along the spine. It read "Melvin" in black ink, and I teared up again. Mrs. Melvin was the reason I chose education as my life's work. It seemed only natural that on the first day of school for the next six years, I called my students to the carpet for their first big announcement of the school year.

I infused celebrations into every facet of our school day because finding something to celebrate with my students reminded them— and myself—that lifelong learning is a celebration of the discoveries, wonderings, and ideas that we sometimes take for granted. I made sure that my students and I gathered during the good times and the not-so-great times because I wanted to instill in them the appropriate and necessary tools to grieve.

Mrs. Melvin had made sure that we were ready to tackle the real world outside of the classroom, and I wanted to do the same for my little ones. And of course, we carried on the tradition of Fun Friday with a contemporary flair that included instructional technology and enrichment on academic topics that were covered the week prior. Students even had the opportunity to develop their own Fun Friday stations. I was determined to carry the torch that Mrs. Melvin had lit so brightly for me and for so many others. The experiences she created on a daily basis went far beyond academics.

She not only taught us how to make good decisions with integrity and honesty, but she modeled that principle every step of the way. Mrs. Melvin differentiated before it became an educational buzzword, and she elevated the importance of socioemotional learning before it was a cornerstone in academics. In her classroom, you were not the label that society or the system assigned to you. You were a human being.

Mrs. Melvin was a pioneer, and she was there, in my heart, as I welcomed my own brood of inquisitive minds, quirky personalities, and lifelong learners into my third-grade classroom.

Three Questions for Conversation

1. How do we ensure that students feel welcome in our schools and communities every single day? How does that investment of time in our students create a connection to deeper learning?
2. Mrs. Melvin was masterful at ensuring students felt valued in the classroom and that they were all celebrated as part of the larger community. How do we authentically celebrate our students and staff so they feel their strengths are valued?

3. What is a practice you use today in your own work that was inspired by a teacher you had when you were a student? How is that past practice still relevant today in our own schools?

MORE ABOUT DR. MARY HEMPHILL

Dr. Mary Hemphill is a leadership expert and coach, K–12 educator and administrator, author, and motivational speaker. With over fifteen years of professional experience as a teacher, administrator, state director, and university professor, Mary understands the importance of fusing education, empowerment, and leadership  together as she works with learning and working communities and speaks to audiences across the country. She holds a PhD in Leadership Studies from North Carolina A&T State University and currently teaches as an adjunct professor at the University of North Carolina at Chapel Hill. Dr. Mary Hemphill is also the CEO and founder of The Limitless Leader, a company that helps individuals ignite the leader in themselves so they can better serve their community, company, and personal career. Mary is the author of *The One-Minute Meeting: Creating Student Stakeholders in Schools*, which teaches readers how to leverage a unique instructional practice called the One-Minute Meeting to authentically glean information from students. You can connect with Mary on either Instagram or Twitter @thelimitlesslady or at her website at bealimitlessleader.com.

5

Fingerprints of Impact:
The Legacy of a Mentor

TOM MURRAY

The delicate balance of mentoring someone is not creating them in your own image, but giving them the opportunity to create themselves.
—Steven Spielberg

During my first year of teaching, I was twenty-one years old, fresh out of college, and thought I had a clue as to what I was getting myself into. I had always wanted to work with kids, and finally, I was getting my opportunity to do so as a brand-new fourth-grade teacher.

Mark Wieder, my mentor and a veteran teacher, taught across the hall in room 303. He had twenty-six years of teaching experience and was the heart and soul of our school. He was brilliant. He was funny. His kids excelled. He was the *exact kind of teacher* I wanted to grow to be. He was the *exact kind of teacher* every kid wanted to learn from.

How do I know?

On my very first day teaching, it seemed as if every student walked into my classroom, hung his or her head a bit, pointed across the hall, and said, "I really wish I had Mr. Wieder this year."

Yes, really.

However, from the moment I met Mark, I understood their disappointment. He was passionate. He was fun. His love for people and for learning radiated in all he did.

For a few minutes before the start of my first day of teaching, Mark and I stood in the hallway and talked. I can still remember my excitement to this day. It just about paralleled the nerves I was feeling at the time.

Just before the bell rang, Mark put his arm around my shoulders, looked at me, and said, "Tom, as your mentor, if there's one thing that I can teach you, it's that this work is about loving and caring about kids. Everything else, and I mean everything else, is secondary to that. It's all about relationships. If you make that the core of all you do, you'll have amazing success in your career. If you lose sight of that, as your mentor, I'll give you two options: get out and go do something different, or refocus on it. The kids who are about to walk down this hallway need you. For some, you may be all they have this year. Don't you ever forget that. Relationships come first; everything else comes second."

The bell rang, and my first set of students walked down the hallway, ready for their first day of fourth grade. Little did I know that what would happen over the course of that school year would fundamentally change who I was as an educator and who I was as a person.

I learned more about connecting with people and loving others in those first few months than I had in any course, in any student teaching experience, or in any previous life experience. I learned what teaching was truly about. My first school year challenged me to my core, altered my mindset, and ultimately set me on a completely different path.

It began with that first class of students. I loved them like my own, but they were a difficult group. As they had in previous years, many of them struggled with their behavior. (In all fairness, as a brand-new teacher, I'm sure I also struggled with all I had to learn.)

From across the hall, I'd watch Mark. His kids laughed often, as did he. In the morning, kids ran to him. It seemed that every afternoon when the bell rang, people came back to visit him. There's this one Friday afternoon that I still remember vividly decades later.

A young couple, carrying their baby, walked down the hallway toward Mark's room. I remember glancing at them and assuming that they were the parents of one of his students. I'd soon learn that they weren't, and I even remember where I was sitting when I heard their conversation.

"Mr. Wieder! Mr. Wieder," the man said, waving from the back of the room. "I'm Sam. I was in your class twenty years ago. Do you remember me?"

Immediately, Mark responded, "Sam! Of course, I do! Come on in!"

Sam looked at his wife, smiled, and said, "Honey, this is the teacher I've always told you about. Mr. Wieder. That's him!" I watched in awe as Mark walked to the back of the room, gave Sam a huge hug, and then introduced himself to Sam's wife.

"Mr. Wieder," Sam said with a nod at the infant in his wife's arms. "This is our baby girl. She's five months old now. We're here visiting my parents for the weekend, so I wanted her to meet my favorite teacher."

Here I was, a twenty-one-year-old kid. Mark had this man as a student the year after I was born. I heard Mark share what he remembered about Sam as a student two decades earlier. I watched in awe. Would that ever be me? Would students remember me and my classroom years later as they did his? Would students want to come back and visit me? Would I leave that type of legacy? Would I be the kind of teacher they'd tell their children about decades later?

As those first few weeks went on, I watched Mark lead. When he walked into the faculty room, people smiled. He'd make everyone laugh. Never once did I hear Mark complain. He brought his best every single day, and it showed. Mark practiced what he preached to his students. They loved him for it, and so did our team.

Meanwhile, across the hall, I was simply trying to survive. Like any new teacher, I was having a hard time just keeping my head above water. I wasn't concerned about long-term planning. I was more concerned about being ready for tomorrow. Sometimes, my only goal was to make it through the day. My students had a tremendous set of needs, and each day seemed to bring a different challenge. I was inexperienced, and many times, I'm sure it really showed.

It was October of that first year when I lost it. I felt like I had exhausted every option with one particular student. Deep down, I knew I was failing. I completely lost my cool in the faculty room one day during lunch. After a frustrating morning, I walked in, huffing and puffing, and threw myself into a chair.

I slammed my hand on the faculty room lunch table and blurted out, "He's not getting it! He's not changing. I hold him in for recess almost every day. I call home almost every day, and his mom never even calls me back. He's disrespectful. He doesn't listen. He does what he wants. I can't deal with this kid anymore."

On the verge of tears, I stood back up and walked quickly out of our faculty room, letting the door close behind me.

I didn't realize it at the time, but Mark had stood up, left his lunch on the table, and followed me back down the hall to my classroom. My mentor opened my classroom door and closed it behind him.

He walked toward me, looked me straight in the eye, and said, "Tom, don't you ever, ever do that again. You want to get through to him? You need to love him. You need to care for him. You need to show him, every day, how much he matters. When he knows how much he matters, maybe then he'll start to show you he cares."

But Mark wasn't done. "What did I tell you before that first day?" he asked. "This work is all about relationships. This work is about loving and caring about kids. Without it, you have nothing. And right now, with this student, it looks like you have nothing. Instead of holding him in for recess, what if you asked him to have lunch so you could get to know him? Instead of yelling at him, what if you encouraged him the moment you saw a positive? Instead of calling home when he got into trouble, what if you called home for something great? When do you think he last heard a compliment? When do you think his mom last received a positive call home? If you want to get through to him, Tom, maybe it's you who needs to change."

Humility instantly set in. It was the lowest moment of my young career and ultimately one of the most humbling moments I'd ever have as an educator. Tears streamed down my face as we stood together in my classroom that October afternoon. After some needed (and deserved) harsh words, Mark stepped toward me, and this amazing teacher of twenty-six years leaned in and gave me a hug.

I realized at that moment that he, too, had become emotional. His heart truly ached for me. He desperately wanted me to succeed.

Mark then softly whispered, "You can do this, Tom. I believe in you."

He was spot-on. My heart was the one that had hardened. I was the one who needed to change.

It was in that moment that faith overcame fear. It was in that moment that empathy overcame a hard heart. It was in that moment that I realized relationships needed to be the foundation of this work.

Later that year, I learned that the child I'd struggled to reach had been the victim of one of the worst abuse cases I'd see in my entire career. That was the reason. When I began to take the time to see his heart and understand his story, I was no longer blinded by my own shaded lens. Just getting to school in the morning was an accomplishment for this precious boy. Here I was, so focused on me that I couldn't see him. I was so focused on my needs, and him conforming to my rules and my ways of doing things, that I had completely missed looking at his heart and what it was that he really needed.

Mark had been right. I will forever be glad that I had a colleague, a true mentor, who called me out, man-to-man, and set me straight. He didn't gossip about my shortcomings in the faculty room. He coached me and set me straight when needed. He gave insight into what would work. His experience, thoughtfully woven by his courage and willingness to help, would change the course of my career, and it was exponentially compounded by what would happen next.

As the months went on, my respect for Mark grew. I watched as he asked our principal if he could take the first few minutes of a faculty meeting to lead a fun activity for the team. I watched him dress up for assemblies to make kids laugh and have fun. I watched as he created the type of classroom where kids wanted to be. He had high expectations for and loved every one of his students, and they thrived.

I no longer wondered why every fourth grader wanted to be a part of his class. Mark's kids were loved. They were challenged. He believed in each one of them—hundreds of them over the years. Mark made the experience for them personal and authentic. The relationships Mark had with his kids, and the way he fostered an inclusive culture, made them feel like they belonged and could change the world. His relationships were the foundation of the success that continuously occurred in that classroom.

Mark was irresistible to others, students and staff alike. And it had nothing to do with his number of steps on the pay scale, the bulletin boards that he hung, or how pretty his handouts may have looked. Everybody loved him for the personal and authentic person he was. We loved how he treated others and how he put relationships and loving others at the heart of all he did.

Over the next few months, learning from Mark and other amazing, experienced colleagues, I began to change my practice. My confidence increased. I finally felt like maybe, just maybe, I could do this teaching thing.

As I changed my own mindset, my students responded, exactly as Mark said they would. The experience of a veteran teacher is invaluable, and Mark's wisdom guided me as only a true mentor could. My heart softened. When I changed my mindset from what I taught to who I taught, the real work came into focus. I began to understand the immense connection between personal and authentic relationships and student-learning outcomes.

As my attitude improved, so did my students' behavior.

As my love for them grew, so did their respect and concern for me.

As my heart opened, I could finally pour into their lives.

As a team, working through things together, we began to win.

Teachers are the only people on the planet who go to bed worrying about other people's children. Early on, I'd go to bed and stare at the ceiling, stewing in frustration from the day. Months later, I'd still lose a tremendous amount of sleep but for entirely different reasons. I'd gained immense empathy for all that my children had on their plates, all they dealt with at home, and all the things I took for granted in life, for which their little hearts longed.

Things were looking up. And that's when tragedy struck.

The next few months would be some of the most difficult that I had ever encountered. My core would be shaken, my confidence rattled, my heart broken. I would question over and over again if I had enough courage to be a teacher. I often wondered if I had a strong enough heart to work with kids.

It was the Wednesday before spring break, and we had an early dismissal that afternoon. The previous night, Mark and his wife, Rae Ann, had picked up the fourteen-foot camper that they had just purchased. He had such excitement in his voice as he showed me the pictures from the brochure and told me all about it that day.

"Check this part out, Tom. We can put the grill back here. The bedroom is back here," he went on.

After school that day, Mark was heading home to pick up his wife for a trip to Maryland, where they'd watch their son, Mark Jr., play tennis at college. I was excited for them. As we stood in the hallway that afternoon and wished each other a great long weekend, I waved and said, "Have a great time, Mark! Enjoy the new camper. Have a safe trip. I'll see you on Tuesday."

Those would be my last words to Mark. But in that moment, I didn't realize it'd be our last conversation. I didn't realize in that moment that I had just said a final goodbye to my mentor.

If only I could have said thank you one more time.

The following morning, I walked outside to get the local newspaper. I slid it out of the newspaper box at the end of my driveway and looked down at the front-page headline: Couple from Macungie Killed in Fiery Accident on Turnpike. I quickly scanned the article.

"A sport utility vehicle pulling a trailer ran out of control and skidded off the Northeast Extension of the Pennsylvania Turnpike south of the Quakertown interchange, catching fire and killing a Macungie couple Wednesday afternoon. Mark Alton Wieder, 48, and Rae Ann Wieder, 50, both of 30 S. Sycamore St., were killed, state police at King of Prussia said."

Only those who have experienced sudden tragedy with loved ones can understand the fear, the anger, the disbelief, and the raw emotion that ensues in moments like these.

In that moment, my mentor, an amazing husband, dad of two, family man, and one of the best teachers to ever walk this earth, and his loving wife, were gone. Like so many others, I was heartbroken. No, heartbroken didn't begin to describe the grief felt by those who knew the couple.

That afternoon, many of my colleagues came together at school to mourn the loss of our friend. With heavy hearts, we shared stories of the man he was. We cried together. We loved on one another, holding each other's hearts in our hands.

I've come to realize that you never really know when a final moment will happen. You only know once the moment has passed and reality has become a memory.

The last smile.

The last high five.

The last hug.

The last goodbye.

Mark's life was cut way too short. Yet during his forty-eight years, he fully lived. He made the most of each and every day. Mark had more joy and found more happiness through his relationships in forty-eight years than many feel in longer lifetimes. He epitomized the true impact of a teacher.

I'm not sure if Mark ever grasped the actual impact he had as a teacher, the legacy he built, or the lives he changed, including mine. Sometimes I wonder if we'll ever really know how long our fingerprints, as educators, will last on those we have the privilege to serve. Mark's fingerprints endure on the lives of those he touched, and through them, his impact will last for generations.

Never say that you are *just* a teacher. You have the opportunity, every day, to change the lives of kids. Just like my mentor, Mark Wieder, did for over two and a half decades.

Mark's passing helped me understand that the quality of our relationships dictates our personal happiness. Ultimately, our success is solidified and authenticated by these relationships. For Mark, these relationships were plentiful. They were personal in nature. They were authentic in experience. They were the foundation of all he did, both at home and at school. They are where his legacy will live.

The work is hard. The work is stressful. The work is emotional. But our kids are worth it.

Three Questions for Conversation

1. How would you design a student learning experience if the quality of the relationship was at the core?
2. Share an experience where your mindset shifted once you finally understood the story behind the situation. How did this learning experience help the next time you faced a similar challenge?
3. Think of a colleague who has impacted your practice today. What lessons did you learn and how did you replicate them in your own work and learning?

MORE ABOUT TOM MURRAY

Tom serves as the director of innovation for Future Ready Schools, a project of the Alliance for Excellent Education in Washington, DC. He has testified before the United States Congress and has worked alongside that body and the U.S. Senate, the White House,  the U.S. Department of Education, state departments of education, corporations, and school districts throughout the country to implement student-centered, personalized learning while helping to lead Future Ready Schools and Digital Learning Day. Murray serves as a regular conference keynote speaker and was named the 2017 Education Thought Leader of the Year, one of 20 to Watch by the National School Boards Association, and the 2015 Education Policy Person of the Year by the Academy of Arts and Sciences. His book, *Learning Transformed: 8 Keys to Designing Tomorrow's Schools, Today,* was published by ASCD in 2017, and his latest book, *Personal & Authentic: Designing Learning Experiences that Impact a Lifetime,* was released in 2019. Both are best sellers. Connect with him at thomascmurray.com.

PART II

Who Is an Administrator Who Inspired You and Why?

6

When Someone Believes in You First

GEORGE COUROS

If your actions create a legacy that inspires others to dream more, learn more, do more, and become more, then you are an excellent leader.
—Dolly Parton

I had no interest in ever becoming a school administrator. Sure, I hoped to be a leader. But as any educator will tell you, many incredible educational leaders aren't always the ideal administrator. And not all administrators are leaders. I wanted to be someone worth following, but the way I saw it, school administration was not in my career path.

Finding the Best Ideas through Differing Perspectives

In the middle of summer one year, I found myself with an unexpected opportunity. My principal at the time, Kelly Wilkins, was trying to coax me into applying for an assistant principal position.

Strangely enough, I decided to give it a try. I still didn't want to be an administrator, but I figured I could learn from the experience of going through the process. Perhaps I would get an interview and then later apply for positions that would better fit my strengths and current aspirations. (To be clear: not administration.)

I couldn't believe it, but I got the interview. Looking back, I realize I probably got the opportunity because the job was posted in the middle of summer. Most people interested in that type of position were likely hired earlier in the year or weren't scouring job postings because they didn't think anything would become available over the summer. Part of me thinks I landed the interview because of a lack of candidates, but when opportunity knocks, you have to be willing to answer the door.

I can tell you this—as I entered the room for my interview, I wasn't nervous at all. Not because I was overconfident, but perhaps the opposite. I expected to get the job about as much as I'd expect to win a game of one-on-one with Michael Jordan. I was going to walk in and give it my best, learn from the experience, and enjoy the opportunity.

There were two people in the interview room as I entered. One was the head of human resources, and the other was the current principal, Archie Lillico. We exchanged niceties and went through the typical questions, covering my educational experience and a little bit about my background. I don't remember what happened, but those niceties quickly evaporated.

In what felt like an out-of-body experience, I was arguing with Archie about educational philosophy. When I say "arguing," I don't mean "disagreeing." I mean fighting in a way I would fight with someone in my family. The head of HR shifted into referee mode, making sure things didn't get out of hand.

Weirdly, though there was a challenge in the moment, there was also a level of comfort. At the end of the interview, we shared pleasantries, the sort of remarks you would make to a bad date or to someone you knew you would never see again. I acted nicely, but I knew this was not going to go anywhere.

After the interview, I called my current principal and said, "I have no idea what just happened, but I started arguing with the principal during the process, and it was easily the worst interview I've ever had."

Kelly said to me, "Trust me, that is just Archie. He's a really good guy."

I really liked Kelly, but I was thinking, *You are underestimating how badly this went!*

About forty-eight hours after the interview, I received what I thought was the obligatory "you didn't get the job, but thanks for coming" phone call from Archie. I greeted him with an awkward hello, hoping that he would not confirm that I had the worst interview in the history of interviews. That didn't happen.

Archie shared that while we had argued in the interview, I was the only person who had challenged him. And that was what he was looking for in an assistant principal. He didn't need someone who thought like him—he'd be there for that. He was interested in hiring me because he needed someone who thought differently, as long as at the end of the day, we both had the same goal of serving the needs of kids.

You know in cartoons when a character's jaw drops to the ground in pure amazement? My reaction to the offer probably looked a lot like that.

I was really confused and asked, "Why would you want that?" He told me that it was his first year at that school, and he wanted to do really well in his job. If he was doing something wrong, he wanted to hear it from me first, not after the fact from students, teachers, and parents.

He said, "Your job is to make sure that if you disagree with me, you tell me before I share my plans with others. I don't need someone to agree with me if they think I'm wrong. I need to make the best possible decisions for the community, and that takes different perspectives and insights."

That made sense to me.

In fact, it was a way better way of doing our work. When I first became a principal, I hired people to my leadership team who I knew would disagree with me or see things in a different way and who might be able to connect with the people I had trouble connecting with. Like Archie, I didn't need clones of myself; I needed people who shared my goals but had different perspectives and ideas.

Archie and I had a ton of disagreements in our time together, and that made us both better at our work. Isn't that the point of education? Shouldn't we want to learn new ideas and take actions to best grow in our pursuits?

I hadn't wanted to be an administrator, but I learned something in my new role. Archie didn't hire me to be an administrator; he hired me to be a leader who happened to be in the role of assistant principal. And the most surprising thing of all was that I loved being an assistant principal and working with Archie.

I often joke that being an AP is the best job in the world because you have a ton of authority to make things happen, but if you screw up, everyone blames the principal. Archie taught me lessons that I applied not only to my administrator journey but also to my personal life. Bits of Archie's wisdom guided me in fatherhood, as well.

In fact, though I worked with him directly for only two years, I still call him about my own children's experiences in school. I know he always keeps kids' best interests at the forefront of his decision making. That, and I know he will tell me if he thinks I am being an idiot. Those are the kinds of people I need in my life.

But I wouldn't have met Archie, become an administrator, or even been involved in education today if it wasn't for Kelly Wilkins.

Believing in Yourself

To be writing any story about how I became an administrator is surreal to me, and not because my younger self didn't believe in his ability to reach that rung of the career ladder. No, I simply hadn't been interested in administrative positions. And, to be honest, I didn't expect to be in education long enough to change my mind.

At that time in my life, I was so disenchanted with teaching. I had lost my passion for the work and was planning my exit out of education. I'd taken to job searching in fields outside of education.

Within one year, I went from not wanting to be an educator to not being able to envision leaving the profession. All it took was one person to get me to see something I hadn't seen in a while, if ever. That person was Kelly Wilkins.

Through a series of serendipitous circumstances, I ended up in an interview for a middle school teacher position. The job title had been vague at best. I wasn't interviewing for a "middle school math" or "grade six teacher" position; I'd applied for a general "middle school teacher" role. I was a little nervous to apply for the position—I didn't want to end up in a job that required teaching content that I wasn't familiar with—but I decided to try anyway. I knew I could always say no if it didn't seem like a good fit. I needed a change and figured this opportunity might help.

As I entered the interview room, I was greeted by the same human resources leader who would later referee my interview with Archie. She led me into another room, handed me a sheet of paper, and asked me to review it. On it was a list of approximately fifteen topics. The instructions simply stated, "Feel free to talk about any of these ideas in the interview." This was different than what I was used to, but it was interesting.

I didn't wait long before Kelly and her assistant principal, Carolyn Cameron, arrived. What followed was one of the quickest hours of my life. We talked about the things that made me passionate and the things that excited me. It felt less like an interview and more like a conversation about education with colleagues in a staff room. Looking back on it, I realize that was intentional. The typical interview process doesn't happen often in our everyday practice, but those conversations do. How we interact in those spaces really matters.

The conversation was like a great movie on teaching. We laughed, we cried, and we talked about our passions for education. I left the room with more energy than I had when I first entered.

I was offered the job, and although I really loved the connection we made, I was actually hesitant to accept. I still wasn't sure if I wanted to be involved with education at this point in my life. In the end, I took the job and gave myself one year to see if a change of scenery would make a difference. But I also decided not to let my past experiences affect this new position. I had entered into a job with a totally blank slate. This was a new school, new division, new staff—new everything—and I didn't want to *just* make a good impression; I wanted to make an impression that lasted.

When we discussed the requirements of the job, I realized that the listing was so general because Kelly wasn't looking for the best "math teacher" or best "sixth-grade teacher." She was looking for the best person for her school, and she knew she could adjust teaching assignments to bring out the best in her people. Kelly fitted the job to my strengths while filling a need that she believed the school had at that time.

This wasn't a one-off occurrence. And it wasn't a special circumstance for me. Kelly never looked for the best teacher at a specific position; she always looked for the best person and fit the position to them.

After a few short weeks of being on her staff, I had already changed my attitude toward education. She saw things in me that I hadn't seen in myself and brought out talents and gifts I didn't even know I had at the time. On more than one occasion, I found myself in the midst of the kind of work I usually moaned about only to realize I wore a giant smile on my face. I would think, *How did she get me to do this?*

By valuing me, that's how. Kelly found so many opportunities to empower me and show her belief in me that when I had to do boring or monotonous jobs for her, I knew they were temporary and would not be the norm. I honestly would have done anything for her because she made me, and others on staff, feel valued and important.

I had been hired as the teacher "tech lead" for the school, with math teaching assignments in grades seven through nine. She pulled me aside one day to help her decide how to spend the school's technology budget for that year. I laughed and said, "That is not something I should do because I am not an administrator."

To which she quickly replied, "George, we hired you for your expertise in this area, and it wouldn't make sense for me to make that decision. It's not my strength; it's yours."

I was stunned. She didn't lead like other administrators I'd known. In past jobs, I may have held a similar role, but I never made this sort of decision. I had to work with the tools I received, whether I wanted to use them or not. Kelly made a lot of sense. She was asking me, "What things do you need? And based on your expertise, what things would best benefit our staff and students?"

I was incredibly excited at first. Of course, I also felt a bit overwhelmed. Now I wasn't just thinking about what would work best for me; I had to consider what would serve the school as a whole. All of a sudden, my ideas and directions were imperative to the success of the school.

Kelly's simple request affected my outlook in such an eye-opening way. And it taught me something I've taken to heart in my career: people are more likely to lift up things that they not only had input on but also helped to create. Kelly made me feel like I was more than a side character in the story; I had a role in shaping it and telling it to others.

That ownership in my role was the first time I felt like I wasn't "just a teacher." I finally realized that being a teacher was about being part of something bigger. It was my aha moment. For the first time, I felt that I could have a tremendous impact on the lives of my students, colleagues, and community—an effect that would last long past my time in school. That was the feeling I had wanted to replicate for my staff, students, and community when I became an administrator.

Kelly's gift was that she was able to see gifts in others and help to draw them out. Weirdly enough, her staff always had a high turnover rate. But it had nothing to do with dissatisfaction. People would be there for a short time before moving on to leadership roles all over the district and outside the state. I remember her actually being teased that she couldn't keep a teacher on her staff, to which she replied with something along the lines of, "I would rather have a great teacher on my staff for two years than have a not-so-great teacher for ten."

We always tell people that they need to believe in themselves, but Kelly showed me how much easier it is to believe in yourself when someone else believed in you first. Her influence lives on in me and in so many others. Each time I think of her, I'm reminded of the impact that amazing administrators can have on a person and how their influence goes beyond professional duties. My personal life became better because Kelly helped me find the purpose and passion that I had thought was lost.

Do Schools Need Administrators?

Years ago, I got into an argument with a good teacher friend of mine who had said, "Schools do not need principals." Personally, I was bothered by the statement because a) I was a principal at the time and b) a principal had saved my career.

So, I challenged him. "I think you believe this because you have never had a really good principal," I said. "They can make all the difference in a school."

He wouldn't hear it and stuck to his belief. Until he got a great principal.

He then admitted, a bit sheepishly, that I had been right. His new principal had made such an impression on him and his school that he had rethought his position on the topic.

I often ask educators about their own administrators, and I hear answers like this: "They are great! They just stay out of my way and let me do whatever I want!"

I will be honest—I cringe a bit when I hear that, although I do understand why educators so often praise hands-off administrators.

A lot of times, we feel that, as teachers, we have lost autonomy in our jobs and are micromanaged in every single aspect of our work. It's only natural that we crave the exact opposite. I have craved that freedom myself at certain points in my career.

But great administrators won't simply stay out of your way. They'll also make you a better educator. And, yes, sometimes they do that by staying out of your way. Other times, they do it by providing mentorship, often when you didn't even know you needed it. The best teachers are incredible learners, and they want to be pushed to grow, as long as they know the person pushing has their back.

Our students have this same need for a gentle push to learn. And they, too, want reassurance that we have their backs. It begs the question: Does our practice tear down or elevate those that we serve?

Kelly taught me to find the best in others, even when they do not see it in themselves. Sometimes our conversations were full of laughter, other times they were filled with tears. But they always prodded my strengths and made me better at my job.

Archie taught me that a great leader doesn't care if the idea is *your* idea or *my* idea. The point was to seek the *best* idea, no matter where it came from. Only by surrounding ourselves with people who share our goals but offer diverse talents, gifts, and experiences can we effectively find that path.

In the upcoming chapters, you will read stories of great administrators who developed and encouraged educators' talents and passions, making them better leaders for our kids. And that ultimately leads our kids to make the world better than what we can imagine.

I hope you enjoy these stories of great leaders—who also happen to be administrators. Like teachers, they can bring out the best in those they serve.

Three Questions for Conversation

1. When you think of a great administrator, what are some defining characteristics, and how do they benefit your work at any level?

2. When was a time that you felt a colleague brought your strengths to the forefront? How did that happen, and how did it make an impact on you?

3. How does working for a great administrator benefit you in your role? How does it make you better at your job? How does it help you personally?

7

The Power of Compassion and Domino's Pizza

DR. KATIE NOVAK

*A single act of kindness throws out roots
in all directions, and the roots spring
up and make new trees.*
—Amelia Earhart

My first teaching job had a hard stop. I was "nonrenewed," an educator's euphemism for getting axed.

As much as I have accomplished in my career, that fact still stings, like gritty salt on a fresh paper cut. Yet its power isn't only negative. Failure, if you want to call it that, can transform us, drive us, make us want to fight.

I remember the meeting as if it was yesterday. The session had been previously scheduled, a follow-up to an earlier observation. I was ready to take any feedback, use it to grow, and keep getting better at what I loved. I had no idea what I was in for.

When I walked into the room, it was too quiet. The assistant principal, normally friendly and warm, was stone-cold silent. I started to put the pieces together. It was Friday afternoon, and my last class was long gone. Bad news.

She asked me to sit down and handed me a letter. I can still hear the paper snapping between my fingers as I unfolded it. As I scanned the words, she explained that I would not be hired back, a statement she had gotten off her chest in a hurry. I didn't understand what that meant. Was I about to be escorted out of the building by a security guard? I asked whether I had to leave right then, and she explained that I would stay until the end of the year.

"So, I'm fired?" I was completely shocked.

"No," she said succinctly, "nonrenewed."

"But why?" I asked, my voice not betraying how ashamed and hurt I was. Because I was a first-year teacher, she revealed nothing more than the fact that I wasn't a good fit. She seemed as uncomfortable as I was. That night, my fiancé took me to Outback Steakhouse, and I cried into a bowl of baked potato soup. That is a sad, sad meme.

Although my colleagues were supportive, no one on the administrative team reached out to me after that meeting to see how I was doing. It was as if they had politely, yet firmly, closed a door. I was on the outside looking in. I pored over my teacher evaluations, looking for some clue, even a red herring. There had to be some obvious indicator or concern I had missed. Nope. Nada.

Here's some advice: if you are going to nonrenew a teacher, it should not be a surprise. Be clear about the possibility and offer concrete steps for improvement. Most important, if you need to move forward with a nonrenewal, have the grace and the humanity to reach out to check on your educators. No one should be ugly crying into baked potato soup, looking like a contestant on *The Bachelor* who failed to get a rose.

The thing about the meeting that bothered me so much was that I truly liked that assistant principal. Her office had been across from the expansive wall of teacher mailboxes, and when I popped in to pick up the mail, I often stopped to say hello. As a track coach, when I tripped on the track, skinned my knees and hips, and looked like I had been attacked by a pack of wild dogs, she's the one I ran (er, hobbled) to for help.

After the initial shock of getting nonrenewed wore off, I started looking for another teaching position in Southern California. As a high school English teacher, I was a dime a dozen. Even though I applied to every job within thirty miles, I didn't get a single request for an interview. I started to question if being a teacher was a good fit for me seeing as I wasn't "a good fit" for it.

My fiancé was supportive. As we watched episode after episode of *Friends*, we scoured job postings. "Hey, here's one in Del Mar," he said in his Southern drawl. "Maybe let's go down there this weekend and check it out."

A new adventure! My search extended farther and farther, like the ripples of a stone thrown into calm waters. Months went by and nothing. The search extended sixty miles. Eighty miles. I started applying for jobs outside of teaching—college admissions counselor, magazine assistant editor, nonprofit development staff. Panic set in.

Finally, I received a call.

Big Bear Lake is a small, tight-knit community in Southern California celebrated as a four-season mountain lake escape. You can surf the waves on the coast and then drive two hours to ski at Bear Mountain in the winter or hike and fish in the summer. I drove two hours to this little vacation hot spot, snaking around the mountain through the San Bernardino National Forest, flanked by perilous drops on both sides, and wondered what on earth I was doing. My friends—my life—were hours away.

I interviewed with the high school principal, a smart and poised woman named Laurie Bruton. I was honest about being nonrenewed, as I didn't want her to find out another way, but shared numerous letters of recommendation from my colleagues, students, and parents.

"Well, that's good news for us," she said, her smile warm. She offered me the job as well as the opportunity to coach varsity volleyball. School started the following week. I was skeptical—and still reeling from the nonrenewal. What if I made the same mistakes, not knowing for sure what those mistakes were? Could I uproot my life for an opportunity that might end with the same disappointment?

Turns out I could.

I accepted the job, packed up all of my belongings, kissed my fiancé goodbye, and moved with my cocker spaniel, Dixin. My fiancé planned to make the transition once he found work.

I rented a cozy A-frame cabin near the base of Bear Mountain, a little ski chalet without any appliances or furniture. Who needed a refrigerator anyway? There was a charming downtown area, Big Bear Village, that looked like it was lifted from a Norman Rockwell painting.

After my first week of teaching and coaching in Big Bear, I couldn't wait to see my fiancé over the weekend. What I didn't expect was for him to drive up in his friend's borrowed pickup truck and break up with me. He had met someone else, and they had been dating for some time. I asked if he wanted the engagement ring back. He shrugged, so I yanked it off my finger and handed it to him.

I sat in the living room on the plush green carpet of the borrowed house—I didn't have a couch yet—and called my parents. My dad encouraged me to make something to eat.

"I don't even have a freaking refrigerator, Dad! There's no food here," I bawled. My dad stayed on the phone with me while I drove to McDonald's to order a cheeseburger and three oatmeal cookies.

I was resolute. "I'm going to resign and come back to New England," I said. "The universe obviously doesn't think I should be a teacher."

My teaching career could have ended there. I was ready to pivot, to find something else. But Laurie Bruton, with her grace and kindness, made an incredible difference in my life. The story I am about to share may seem insignificant, but when I reflect on my journey—sticking with teaching, becoming an administrator, consulting with educators and administrators around the world, and writing books—there is a pin in Big Bear Lake.

My parents convinced me not to resign that evening, and believe me, I took some convincing. I was ready to pack up my red Isuzu Rodeo and drive back to Massachusetts. After I got off the phone with Mom and Dad, I called in to school. I started off cool, "Hi, this is Katie Thibodeau, and I'm not going to be able to come in to work . . ."

I couldn't hold it together and broke down in tears on the answering machine. Not my finest moment, but once I started down that rabbit hole, there was no coming back. I shared how my fiancé left me and how I couldn't come to work and how I wasn't sure about my next steps. I assured whoever would listen to the message that I would send in sub plans. In hindsight, it wasn't the most professional call, but I was only a twenty-two-year-old kid, and I didn't know what else to do.

As administrators, there are moments when we have to decide how we will react. Maybe a colleague shares some bad news. Maybe a staff member challenges our vision. Or maybe a teacher calls out because she's just moved to a new school and her good-for-nothing fiancé decided to ditch her before she even had a chance to buy a couch. Our reactions matter.

I am not sure who checked the school's messages, but whoever it was had the good sense to call the principal. Laurie could have heard that call and questioned her hire. *Oh, dear goodness*, she could have thought, *this kid is a loose cannon.* I thought the same about myself, *How could I teach students when I couldn't even hold myself together for a phone call?*

Within minutes of leaving the message, Laurie called my cell phone. The first thing she said was, "Katie, I am so, so sorry. What a terrible thing to happen." She assured me that she would arrange for a substitute and could even handle the sub plans. I broke down on the phone, heartbroken and also pretty confident I was writing the lines to the sequel in my teaching series: "Katie Nonrenewal 2.0."

When I got off the phone, I sat on the floor like some sad, heart-broken heroine in a bad Hollywood movie. I took my wedding dress out of the closet—my dress for a wedding that would never happen—and took pictures of it so I could sell it on eBay. You couldn't write a more pathetic scene.

The next morning, I woke up alone in Big Bear Lake, exhausted and single for the first time in years. Dixin scratched at the door to go out, but I couldn't imagine going outside—the sun was too bright, the air too crisp. That afternoon, there was a knock at the door. Was it my fiancé? Did he realize he had made a terrible mistake and was about to beg for my undying love and forgiveness? I thank my lucky stars it wasn't. It was Laurie Bruton, the high school principal, with two Dominoes pizzas, one pepperoni and one cheese. She held out the pizzas and asked if I wanted to talk.

I cannot overstate the importance of that moment.

Laurie didn't tell me that things would get better, tell me that someday I would be grateful that he left (which I am!), or ask me when I planned to return to school. Instead, she gave me permission to feel. She delivered lunch, and she told me one thing that I have held close to my heart ever since. "Just promise me this," she said. "Don't make big life decisions when you're not in a good place."

If Laurie had asked me if there was anything she could do, I would have said, "Nothing." I didn't even know how much I needed someone to check on me (or how much my stomach needed those pizzas) until she showed up on my doorstep.

Three days later, I returned to school. I wasn't ready. I returned because I knew I had an administrator who supported me. I returned because those two Dominoes pizzas, and the fact that she literally showed up on my doorstep, showed me that being an educator is one of the most important jobs in the world. With simple decisions—like reaching out to someone in need—we can change the trajectory of their career and their life.

I stayed in Big Bear for the rest of the school year and then I moved back to Massachusetts. I packed up my Rodeo and drove home, Dixin riding shotgun.

I learned so much under Laurie's leadership, and I think of her often. But the most important thing she taught me, by far, was that we have to make time and take action in order to make sure that the people we work with are OK. David Rose, the father of Universal Design for Learning, always said, "Teaching, at its core, is emotional work." Laurie exemplified that for me. She is the reason I am still, and will always be, an educator.

I am so thankful that Laurie Bruton came into my life. I would not be the educator I am today without her. I would not have presented on five continents to tens of thousands of educators about the power of Universal Design. I would not have written nine books about transforming education or collaborated with brilliant practitioners who continue to inspire and push me. I would have not had the opportunity to work directly with clients like Harvard University, the NASA Science Activation Team, the Bill & Melinda Gates Foundation, or the Teaching Channel. Most important, I would not have been hired to consult in the very school district that handed me that nonrenewal letter. How's that for full circle?

Writing this chapter has been therapeutic, a reminder of what I have been through. It has also reminded me of just how much hope and power one person can have. I haven't connected with Laurie since I left Big Bear Lake in 2004. After writing this chapter, I know I need to track her down and thank her for everything. Because that twenty-two-year-old needed a champion. And she got one.

My advice to you is simple. Make sure everyone around you is OK. And if they are not, don't just ask if there is anything you can do. Instead, take action: buy a coffee, send a card, drop off flowers, or if you're feeling like a superstar, order a couple of pizzas.

Three Questions for Conversation

1. Think of a time when you had a huge setback, either personally or professionally. What did you learn from the process? How did it make you better?
2. We all have had colleagues help us when we were struggling. How did someone being there for you personally help you professionally?
3. Teaching is emotional work. What is a way you can "fill someone's bucket" in your work today, and how would that make you personally feel?

MORE ABOUT DR. KATIE NOVAK

Katie Novak, EdD, is an internationally renowned education consultant, author, and adjunct instructor at the University of Pennsylvania. With nineteen years of experience in teaching and administration and an earned doctorate in curriculum and teaching, Katie designs and presents workshops both nationally and internationally, focusing on the implementation of inclusive practices, Universal Design for Learning (UDL), and multitiered systems of support. She is the author of the best-selling book, *UDL Now! A Teacher's Guide to Applying Universal Design for Learning in Today's Classrooms*. Her book *Innovate inside the Box*, cowritten with George Couros, explores how to create innovative and purposeful learning opportunities for students within the constraints of educational systems. Katie's work has been highlighted in many publications, including *Edutopia*, *Language Magazine*, the *Huffington Post*, *Principal Leadership*, *District Administrator*, and *ASCD Education Update*.

— 8 —

He Saw the Me
I Could Be

AMBER TEAMANN

*You can have everything you want in life if you
just help enough people get what they want in life.*
—Zig Ziglar

My goal in life did not include becoming an elementary principal.
Ever.

In fact, it was the furthest thing from my mind as a teacher. If not
for someone I respected seeing potential in me, I wouldn't have had the
opportunities I've had now.

At the time, though, I thought I saw a different opportunity ahead.
After three years in the classroom, I'd finally decided to get my master's
degree in instructional technology. I'd already attended several technology conferences, and it felt *right*. Like this was the path I wanted to
be on.

I transferred to a technology magnet school, not only to utilize
that degree, but also for the chance to work with district-legend Mitt

Price, who was the principal there. Mitt Price had been in our district long enough for everyone to know him and what that campus was able to produce. This was a number of years ago—prior to standardized insanity, although the school was also known for having a very high academic standard.

The pivotal point in my career happened, randomly enough, on a trip to Walmart. Mitt and I were picking up bicycles that I'd arranged to have donated to our Saturday school program, which I was also in charge of. Out of the blue, he said, "You should be a principal."

I laughed it off and said, "No thanks. I've got this degree about done, and it's definitely not in administration." I didn't see myself in his league at all, especially in comparison to his career and all that he had grown and accomplished. He didn't drop it, though, and actually made sure I knew about a certification program that allowed educators with a master's degree to take classes and the admin certification exam. It wasn't an additional degree, but it'd allow me to use what I had already done as a foundation. I'd just need to take the leadership classes and exam.

He went so far as to connect me with a fellow district teacher who had already gone through the program—just to learn the specifics, Mitt said. I reluctantly agreed. I remember telling my husband that maybe this administrative certification would separate me from other EdTech candidates. I probably wouldn't use it to become a principal, but I could use it to advance my career. Little did I know that the characteristics Mitt Price exemplified in his leadership would be the same qualities I'd desperately try to model in my leadership journey.

The way that Mitt motivated students was not only unique but also incredibly memorable. We were a neighborhood magnet school, which meant a certain percentage of students qualified based on test scores, while another chunk came from the surrounding neighborhood. Our methods for motivating students had to be broad and consistent to be able to meet those two different demographic needs.

We had Saturday school. We offered more field trips than any other campus. And as a technology campus, we provided lots and lots of devices. Mitt encouraged his team to do whatever it took to connect with our Beaver Stars, and he set the tone for us all.

I will always remember him throwing a football in the hall with students who just needed a break. That football throwing became an outlet for a student who needed to be up and about, who needed a sensory pause in the school day. I also remember him taking students up on the roof to toss the football and to see the school and neighborhood from above. It was so unlike anything I'd ever seen before that it stood out to me as an adult. They'd go up there and clear off all the toys and balls that had found their way to the roof over time, all while having conversations and building memories. It wasn't a typical reward, but it worked. And it taught me that making memories and setting expectations should be unique.

Mitt made our jobs fun.

He was the king of practical jokes. He wanted educators to enjoy doing their jobs, and one way he did that was by making sure that we laughed. Once, I got an email from our assistant principal asking me to come by her office when I had a chance. Apparently, she wanted to discuss my outfit. The panic that I felt . . .

I didn't know what exactly was wrong with my outfit, but I remember tugging down the hem of my skirt and pulling up my top by the neckline. Did I show too much leg? Was my shirt too low-cut? I taught fourth graders so it wasn't like I wasn't already aware of the need to be professional. *Oh, my goodness*, I thought, *what did I do wrong*?

I walked into her office, stammering and apologizing before she could even speak. She looked up at me, her face blank, and said, "Huh?" In that confused pause, we heard the laughter. I leaned back out of the door and caught Mitt and another teacher in his office nearly collapsing on the floor with hysterical laughter. Our assistant principal learned not to leave her email up when she left the office, and I learned that you could (and should!) have moments of levity while working. You should always take what you do very seriously, but yourself? Not so much.

Mitt made sure that he praised publicly and proudly.

In my last professional transition, when moving files and folders, I came across emails in which Mitt had praised me. Sometimes, he'd hear from other administrators, who reached out to thank me for a training I had done; other times, he'd get a message from a parent who mentioned an interaction with me. He always replied, spoke with praise, and then copied both me and our assistant superintendent. He could have easily just responded to the people who emailed, thanking them for sharing. But instead, he took the time to ensure I felt appreciated.

Just this week, I explained to someone how motivating it was to have him acknowledge the praise or compliment, not just to make sure I knew someone had written him but also to include someone above himself. It's a practice I do today and have heard Dr. Joe Sanfelippo speak about, as well. Recognize, acknowledge, and extend. In doing so, you turn a private moment of praise into a public one.

Mitt helped us set ourselves apart.

As a magnet school, we were trained early and regularly to recruit learners for our program. Our district offered magnet centers: classical arts, advanced academics, and several others. Parents decided what programs would be right for their children. From lesson plans to field trips, our offerings drove our enrollment. We regularly conducted classroom tours. We presented at different learning nights throughout the year. And it was well-known that at any given moment you'd be asked to give your elevator pitch as to what made your classroom and/ or campus unique.

The drive to set ourselves apart each and every day came from Mitt. He didn't lead all the tours, and he didn't give all the speeches. He depended on us for that. We had to individually decide what made us special and sell a family on what we could offer their child. It allowed us to build confidence in our programs and abilities, and helped us see that a classroom of students wasn't a given—it was a gift. I've forgotten what it feels like to want to be the best choice out there, to make sure a family knows that our campus is exactly what their student needs.

Mitt taught us to never stop learning and growing.

I had many opportunities to train, not only with our teachers but also with other campuses, based on some of the strategies and risks I took in our school. I am 100 percent convinced that this professional development led me to my position today, some fifteen years later.

My first conference was one Mitt sent me to as a "reward" for all the extra work he felt I had done as a leader on campus. He didn't push me just to feed my need for growth (though the event certainly helped me grow professionally). He knew that I would bring back knowledge and share it with our staff. Having opportunities to grow my peers was heady stuff for a young teacher.

It was a genius move. He promoted professional development in a way that meant something to me specifically. That moment solidified the fact that teachers need personalized professional development. When you see someone doing something above and beyond, fill their bucket. And fill it in a way that means something to them. I love learning, and he knew that.

Organically ensuring that collaboration and learning went hand in hand benefitted not only me but also our staff and students. Under Mitt's leadership, everyone had opportunities like this. It speaks to one of Mitt's greatest legacies.

Our campus was known for its ability to grow future leaders. If you were to look back on the years that Mitt Price led the school, you would see teachers grow in their careers. One went on to become an assistant superintendent, three became area directors, five became principals, others grew into specialists and coordinators, and I became a director of technology. And those are just the leaders I know about. Were Mitt to document all of the young teachers he grew under his leadership, his legacy would seem limitless.

He helped us see more in ourselves than we ever thought possible. The importance of that skill was, above all else, the greatest takeaway from my time with him. When I met Mitt, I was looking for a direction to go in. Having a confident, secure leader believe in me and point me in the right direction is how I found my forever profession. So far, the very best years of my career—in fact, my entire leadership journey—are a result of the path he turned me toward.

Leaders don't allow their people to languish. Leaders see the next step and the possibility in everyone who serves with them. Mitt never once made me feel like I was just another teacher. He always saw me as more capable than I saw myself, and I will forever be thankful for that.

I've tried to emulate him throughout my career. I take great pride in the number of coworkers whom I have helped to recognize their potential. When I left my last campus, my turnover rate was high, but almost all staff members who left did so because of a promotion they'd earned, a risk they had taken, and the encouragement to take the next step.

Like Mitt, I brag about, lift up, and bring attention to just how amazing the people on my staff are. I am so incredibly proud of those who have moved on to new and exciting opportunities. I may not have had everything to do with them taking the next step in their careers, but I sure am glad I was there to encourage, support, and help wherever I could. Sometimes all you need is someone in your corner cheering for you. I will forever be my staff's champion and Mitt's biggest fan.

Three Questions for Conversation

1. Has your career gone in a direction that you were not expecting? What did you learn from that experience?
2. What are some things in your work that make you enjoy showing up every day? What benefit does that have in improving your work?
3. What are some of the best traits you have seen from a leader, and how have you implemented those same characteristics in your own work?

MORE ABOUT AMBER TEAMANN

Amber Teamann is an administrator turned director of technology and innovation for a growing district outside of Dallas, Texas, Crandall ISD. From a fourth-grade teacher at a public school technology center to her role as a Title I technology facilitator responsi-  ble for seventeen campuses, Amber has helped students and staff navigate their digital abilities and responsibilities. She coauthored *Lead with Appreciation*, a best seller that helps leaders develop and maintain a culture of empowerment and gratitude.

Her educational philosophy and digital portfolio can be found at her website, technicallyteamann.com, and she's on Twitter at @8amber8.

— 9 —

Great Leaders Create More Leaders

DWIGHT CARTER

Your good times will start the minute you start believing in yourself!
—Somya Kedia

People often say that when teachers choose to become administrators, they cross over to the "dark side." Maybe you feel that way. Maybe you've even said it to a fellow teacher. *There goes Sarah. She's crossed over to the dark side.*

Like you, I used to question why anyone would become an administrator. And is it any wonder? Movies portray principals as idiots or mean-spirited jerks. They're the villains of the story and the people to avoid. Even commercials make fun of administrators—think quick-tempered Principal Wilson, who goes off on the PA system when someone parks in his spot (and is, naturally, pacified by a nacho-flavored Kraft Single). While it is hilarious, it also reinforces how some see administrators. It's no wonder people liken the move to administration to a Jedi joining up with Darth Vader.

I used to jokingly make that same statement when I became an administrator to appeal to others. ("Oh, ha ha, it's hilarious how I've defected to the bad guys.") After many years in the position, I hate the statement. It was an administrator who helped change my career. He has been a beacon of light and someone I aspire to be like.

The person you work for can make your job miserable or enjoyable. Leadership makes all the difference in the world.

"Yes, I know who you are. I've heard nothing but great things about you. Nice to meet you! Sit down, and let's talk."

Well, if those weren't just the most reassuring words I'd heard all morning . . .

Let me back up. When I get nervous, my hands and feet sweat profusely. I actually keep a handkerchief in my pocket in case I need to wipe my hands before greeting others. There's nothing worse than a cold, wet handshake! My palms were slick the morning I mustered up the confidence to walk to the main office and introduce myself to Mark White and to my surprise, he uttered those words. Ah, a sigh of relief . . .

Mark was in his first year as principal at Gahanna Lincoln High School, and I was just starting my seventh year in the classroom. I was also finishing up my master's degree in education leadership and had a great mentor in my former principal, Cheri Dunlap.

Cheri had taken a liking to me when I joined the high school staff in 1997. She was brilliant, creative, and a strong leader. One day in the fall of 1999, she tapped me to be a Critical Friends Group facilitator. I never questioned why I was tapped, which I think is more of a gen-erational thing. See, I'm a Gen Xer, and we typically don't ask a lot of questions about why we are asked to do something; we just do it. And when my boss asked me to attend a training, I took it as a directive instead of a question. It's a whole different ball game now, but I digress.

I enjoyed the growth opportunities under Cheri and wondered if they would disappear under the new guy. Would I have to start over? Would Mark White see whatever Cheri saw in me?

I was intimidated, to say the least. Mark had a presence about him. He commanded a room, hence my nerves upon meeting him. But at his warm welcome, I breathed a sigh of relief.

I took a seat facing his desk, and we just talked. He leaned back in his chair, in a relaxed fashion, and asked about my career, family, and aspirations. I told him I was working on my master's degree in education leadership, and he leaned forward and said, "Whatever you need, I will help you." The look on his face and the seriousness in his eyes let me know he meant it. From that moment on, he took me under his wing, and I haven't been the same educator since.

When someone expresses belief in you, you have no choice but to believe in yourself.

Throughout the rest of that year, he and I often talked about leadership and the future of education. He would call me into his office to ask how I would handle a particular situation. At first, I was intimidated because I thought I had to have the "right" answer. Most of the time, I gave him a weak response, and he would make suggestions about things I should consider. And then, just like that, he would walk away to handle another situation, and I would wonder if I got it right.

I watched him closely during staff meetings and saw how he responded to negative comments and reactions. He faced them head-on, unbothered and confident. He modeled strength, collaboration, and clarity. Like the time duty coverages were screwed up.

The staff was in an uproar. People blamed the administration, complaining about the situation and defending how they thought things should go. They criticized the "new guy" and said he didn't know what he was doing. He'd heard it all day long and decided to call a staff meeting after school.

When the meeting began, there were no niceties. He immediately addressed the elephant in the room. I remember his words as if it were yesterday: "You guys don't even know me. I hear your concerns, and we will figure this out. Relax." The silence was deafening. A few hours of work with the assistant principals, and he'd solved the problem and restored order—cool points for Mark.

I was amazed by his approach. He faced the problem head-on, listened to our concerns, worked with others to solve the problem, and communicated with clarity. And he did all that in a timely manner.

The following school year marked a turning point in my career. I didn't know it at the outset, but it would be my last year in the classroom.

One day in late spring, Mark knocked on my classroom door and motioned for me to come into the hallway. Nervous, I excused myself from my students and headed out to see what he needed. He said, "Mr. Andersson just accepted an assistant principal position at Westerville South. You should apply for his position. I know you have a few classes left in your master's program, but it will be a good experience for you."

Stunned, I said I'd think about it and returned to my students. However, there was little teaching going on after that. I couldn't get the conversation out of my head.

The next day, I went to Mark's office to let him know I'd apply for the assistant principal job. Within two weeks, I was sitting in an interview with the HR director, assistant superintendent, and high school assistant principals. I figured I had nothing to lose because I hadn't gotten my administrator license and probably wouldn't get the job anyway. I walked out feeling pretty good about my interview but thought that would be the last I'd hear about the position.

A few days later, Mark again knocked on my door. This time, he had a stern look on his face when he asked me to join him in the hallway. I quickly stepped out of my room and said, "What's wrong?"

"I don't know what you said, but they loved you!" he said. "You have a second interview tomorrow. Greg (the superintendent) will be there with several district and building administrators. Will you be ready?"

I nodded my head, and immediately my hands and feet began to sweat. But I had nothing to worry about. Turns out it wasn't an interview but a job offer!

From the moment I accepted the position, Mark mentored and coached me. We talked almost every day. When I made a mistake while disciplining a student or mishandled a teacher's concern, he always started with, "So, what did you learn? What will you do differently?" Every moment was a teachable moment.

Great leaders create more leaders, not more followers.

I was an assistant principal with Mark for three years until I became principal at a middle school in the same district. I was able to apply some of the principles and strategies I learned from him in my own building. It was my chance to see if I could be a great leader apart from my mentor. I developed my own leadership skills, taking ideas from Mark, Cheri, Keith Bell, and a few other administrators I knew.

Mark and I collaborated on several district initiatives, such as Understanding by Design, differentiated instruction, and formative assessment. We'd bounce ideas off each other, and I'd glean nuggets of wisdom about how to lead change. He continued to push me to think about the future of education and what schools could look like for kids. He saw a much more open, fluid, and student-centered education system—one that is entirely different from our current model.

When he moved into the assistant superintendent position, I applied for the high school principal position. Once again, Mark and I were working together, he as the assistant superintendent and I as the principal of the largest high school in Central Ohio.

I was in my early thirties when I became a high school principal. I was also a former teacher and assistant principal at that school, so I was nervous about returning. Mark knew this and said, "Dwight, just be yourself. You got the position because you are good at what you do. You are ready."

On the first day of the new school year, I decided to reintroduce myself to the staff since they knew me as a former colleague and assistant principal. I had many friends there who I'd grown up with professionally. My connections were deep, and the stakes were high. There was lots of anticipation and high expectations.

I couldn't help but wonder how I would fill Mark's shoes. He may have started as the new guy, but long before he left, the staff had grown to love him. As I prepared for my first meeting with the staff, I heard Mark's words: "Just be yourself. You got the position because you are good at what you do . . ."

By the end of the meeting, the staff was laughing, crying, cheering, and applauding. I shared my vision of education through stories. I connected with their heads and their hearts. I celebrated their successes and challenged them to paint a picture of what more we could do. By the end of the meeting, they knew I was the right person for the job, and I earned it on my merit.

Leaders share a vision. Vision frustrates our present but excites our future.

My new school wasn't the idyllic high school of Hollywood. We had over twenty-four hundred students and were at capacity. The hallways were narrow and crowded, classrooms were full, and we were simply out of space.

Mark and I started having conversations about the building with the superintendent, Greg Morris. We discussed the prospect of a new high school building, but the community or other stakeholder groups didn't want that. Mark had an idea that seemed nearly impossible.

Adjacent to the high school was an old, abandoned Kroger supermarket. He posed the question, "Why not buy the property and build a high school annex?"

We answered another, unspoken question: Why not explore Mark's vision? So, we did. Mark led book studies of authors like Daniel Pink, Thomas Friedman, and Ian Jukes. We brought Ian Jukes in to talk to the high school staff about the future of education and see what could be possible. We launched a professional development plan to explore how colleges and businesses created open spaces with modular furniture and color to encourage creative and critical thinking, collaboration, and problem-solving skills. Through community partnerships, teamwork, professional development, and open forums with staff, students, and community members, Clark Hall was born.

It took a whole lot of hard work to get us there though. Mark introduced us to many authors to challenge our thinking and help us envision a different model for another generation of students. When Ian Jukes visited, he talked with the staff about the future of work and what students need in order to learn to thrive globally. We continued to attend the annual Model Schools Conference to learn from futurist Dr. Bill Daggett. We constantly challenged our staff to think of different, more creative ways to do school.

Mark would always ask us, "What will school look like in the years 2030, 2040, and 2050?" Heck, I was focused on the upcoming staff meeting or observations I needed to finish. Who had time to think that far ahead?

Those forward-thinking prompts were part of Mark's genius. But while the building was his brainchild, it was also a collective effort.

We got the students involved in the naming process. Teachers helped select the colors and furniture and toured colleges and businesses to see how they designed their spaces to encourage creativity, critical thinking, and collaboration. Mark spearheaded all of this.

Leaders expose others to what is possible and then create the conditions for them to grow.

Mark connected us with two dynamic professors, Betsy Hubbard (@BetsyHubbard) and Debra Jasper (@Debrajasper) from the Ohio State University's Kiplinger Program of Journalism. He shared the vision for Clark Hall with them and discussed our need to expose people to our school's great work. It was 2010, and social media had exploded.

On April 29, 2010, I joined three other building principals at an intense, three-day social media boot camp called Kip Camp. There we met Debra and Betsy, the coordinators and facilitators of Kip Camp.

It was an incredible experience that exposed me to the world of social media. We discussed how businesses used Facebook, the importance and influence of blogging, and the use of Twitter, among other Web 2.0 tools. Before this, I saw no use for Twitter whatsoever. I didn't care what or where celebrities ate for breakfast or how they dressed for some awards show. I certainly didn't care about the random pieces of information I assumed people tweeted!

So, when Debra and Betsy spent the second day of the three-day camp talking about Twitter, I was not thrilled. But I was intrigued. I saw the possibilities of connecting with people all over the world through Twitter. I learned the language and the basics of how to compose a message in a hundred and forty characters. I learned about hashtags, how to DM, RT, and follow someone. It was a great experience, but to say that I was overwhelmed would be an understatement. I left day two of Kip Camp enthused but not yet sold that I would or could use Twitter as a principal. There were so many rules, policies, and fears surrounding social media and public education.

On the third day, I played with Twitter a little more and stumbled upon Shelly Terrell-Sanchez and the Teacher Reboot Camp. I immediately followed her. Before long, I'd stumbled upon accounts for George

Couros (@gcouros) and Connected Principals (@conprin), followed by Tom Whitby (@tomwhitby) and The Educators PLN.

It was like the scales had been removed my eyes. Tweets about emerging and relevant educational issues were nonstop, and I couldn't read them fast enough. I hadn't realized this world even existed!

As I leaped into the Twitterverse, I first only lurked, reading others' tweets without replying, retweeting, or contributing in any way. But about a month into it, I began to reply to tweets, comment on blogs, and retweet information. I gained so much more from Twitter once I began to contribute.

At that time, I discovered a concept that many education tweeters referred to as a Personal Learning Network. A PLN is a network of educators who learn from one another regardless of distance and time. I was hooked!

Through Twitter, I was exposed to education conferences, Teach Meets, and "unconferences" that occurred worldwide. I even participated in my first online education conference—for free. Talk about relevant and engaging professional development!

I have communicated with educators from Canada, Australia, New Zealand, Indonesia, England, China, and all over the United States through Twitter. I am so thankful to members of my PLN for adding to my growth as an educator. At no other time in my career had I the privilege to learn from so many different people from so many walks of life.

Leaders broaden our idea of what is possible and then pave the way for us to thrive. Mark did that for me. As a result, we have coauthored three books about our journey as education leaders, from challenging the status quo of school design to providing a way for leaders to face disruptions.

Because of Mark, I am the educator I am today. It's worth repeating: when someone expresses belief in you, you have no choice but to believe in yourself.

Three Questions for Conversation

1. Think of someone who believed in you in your career. What impact did that have on you personally and professionally?

2. Great leaders create more leaders, not followers. What opportunities do you have to lead in your community? What opportunities do your colleagues or students have to lead because of your mentorship?

3. What is your vision for the future of your own classroom or school community? What supports would you need to make that vision a reality?

MORE ABOUT DWIGHT CARTER

Dwight Carter is a nationally recognized school leader with nearly thirty years of experience. Because of his collaborative and innovative leadership, he was inducted into the Jostens Renaissance Educator Hall of Fame in 2010. He was also named the 2013 National Association of Secondary School Principals' Digital Principal of the Year, the 2014 Academy of Arts and Sciences Education High School Principal of the Year, the 2015 Ohio Alliance of Black School Educators Principal of the Year, and a 2021 Columbus Africentric Early College Sankofa Emerging Leader Award winner. He is currently an assistant director at Eastland Career Center in Groveport, Ohio.

He is the coauthor of three books: *What's in Your Space?: 5 Steps to Better School and Classroom Design* (Corwin, 2015), *Leading Schools in Disruptive Times: How to Survive Hyper-Change* (Corwin,

2017), and the second edition of *Leading Schools in Disruptive Times* (Corwin, 2021). You can connect with Dwight on Twitter at @Dwight_Carter or on his blog, dwightcarter.edublogs.org.

— 10 —

Designing the Culture for Learning and Innovation

DR. KATIE MARTIN

Culture is not the most important thing;
it's the only thing.
—Jim Sinegal

During the 2013–2014 school year, I was on Washington Middle School's campus regularly. I was supervising teacher candidates at a local university, and as the newest member of the team, I was placed at Washington—the most challenging of schools.

I vividly remember walking down halls marked with yellow caution tape, the lines indicating which side of the hallway the kids were expected to walk. I immediately felt anxious about following the right path, and I could only imagine how the students felt. I watched them navigate the cold halls as teachers yelled at them to stay in line.

In the majority of classrooms, rows of desks and compliance-based structures were the norm. The teachers followed textbooks that few students had the skills (or desire) to read independently. Staff expressed to me that they were stressed and burned-out, which, frankly, was evident from their actions.

The middle school students were well below grade level. Most were disengaged, and some acted out as a result. It was heartbreaking, and it is an all-too-common example of underperforming schools.

Toward the end of the school year, I noticed a change in the tone of some of the teachers. The teacher candidates and those on campus had a slightly different level of excitement and energy. They told me about a committee that was working on the magnet school petition. As I observed classes and debriefed teachers, I tried to learn more about the change happening at Washington Middle School.

What I uncovered had a lot to do with the new guy on campus. He was hard to miss, sporting orange sunglasses and Vans. This, I found out, was the new principal, Dr. Eric Chagala. And under his leadership, Washington Middle, a Title I school that had chronically underperformed—with 98 percent of its students receiving free or reduced lunches and about 80 percent of its students in the ESL program—was closing its doors at the end of the year.

The following year, Vista Innovation and Design Academy (VIDA) was born.

When Dr. Chagala and the staff opened VIDA's doors, students and educators encountered the facility with an entirely new approach. All of the teachers were given the choice to leave, but because they had worked collaboratively to develop the new school model and created a shared understanding of the vision, all but one of them opted to stay. (That teacher eventually asked to return.)

Now, this rate of retention is rare for schools that aren't going through such a radical change. For a school experiencing a complete transformation? It is unheard-of. But the staff members believed in what they were doing and wanted to come together to create a new culture that valued learning, supported innovation, and met the needs of their community. Remember, these were the same teachers who felt they couldn't reach their students and who were tired and burned-out. They chose to stay and be part of a new school model with the same students because they believed in the mission they had helped create.

Redefining the School Culture

As a dynamic leader, Dr. Chagala has worked tirelessly to ensure that VIDA—which means *life* in Spanish—is not only a name. He and his team strove to create a campus culture that breathes life into everyone it serves. He will also be the first to tell you that this endeavor isn't a one-person job. He has leveraged community and business partnerships to learn, and tapped teachers and students to help shape the culture. The school is rooted in caring and nurturing learners in an environment that utilizes design thinking as a core strategy for learning and improvement. Teachers, parents, students, and community members all play an integral role in shaping and upholding the culture.

The school's website states, "We dare to ignite the creative genius in each student by kindling their unique strengths, interests, and values as we utilize the design thinking process as a common framework to solve problems across all disciplines."

What makes this school unique is that its mission highlights a focus on individuals finding their passions through an interdisciplinary approach, and its programs align with the mission. To ensure teachers have the expertise and mindsets to "ignite creative genius" in their students, they have opportunities to learn and model these same values to students.

The staff and community learn and solve problems together. The VIDA community of staff and families came together to determine the school's core values, known as their GILLS.

Their mascot is a shark, an animal whose gills allow it to breathe and give it life. In the same way, the school's GILLS breathe life into its mission. They remind leaders and learners that VIDA prizes these core values:

Grit to persevere. *We never give up.*
Innovating through design. *We create solutions.*
Learning about empathy. *We seek to understand the viewpoints of others.*
Leading with integrity. *We make a positive impact.*
Sparking creativity. *We honor imagination.*

Designing a culture that would build the skills, knowledge, and mindsets that they espoused in their GILLS wasn't an easy order. Dr. Chagala and his team had to rethink how they see learners and adjust their approach to design learning experiences.

We can't change *who* we serve, but we can change *how* we serve them. During the summer, the teachers partnered with community members to paint the building, resulting in a learning environment that matched VIDA's newfound philosophy and culture. They didn't change everything overnight or even over the course of the full year. They freely admitted it was a work in progress, but they continue to work together and focus on learning new approaches and improving to meet the needs of their unique population.

In the first months of school, attendance was up, referrals were down, and smiles permeated the building. I visited VIDA shortly after it opened, and I stay connected to the work it does by following @VidaSharks on social media. The yellow caution lines are gone, and in their place are halls that lead to inspiring places such as design studios, where students have opportunities to make and create based on a variety of challenges. Today, students share ideas in their classes, and teachers experiment with a variety of new strategies. Artwork covers the walls, and students meet in classrooms, courtyards, and hallways to work with each other on various projects.

When I last toured the school, students gladly shared what they were working on and learning. I couldn't help but smile at the dramatic changes I saw on campus as Dr. Chagala, who has since become a dear friend, proudly shared what his staff and students were doing.

In 2021, eight years after VIDA opened, attendance is still up, scores continue to increase, and most important, the students, staff, and community know they matter. It's a place where learners are fighting to get in rather than out. The example and the work happening at VIDA highlight that, although we can't change who we serve, we can change how we serve them. Check out their video at bit.ly/wearevida.

VIDA's example makes one thing clear: if our schools aren't working for those we serve, we can no longer accept that *they* need to change. We must consider how we can change to best serve them.

Professors Bill Lucas and Guy Claxton explain that intelligence is made up of a number of complex attributes that are shaped by how and what we learn. Teachers who actively cultivate broader definitions of *smart*—and who strive for better opportunities to learn, for both themselves and their students—have demonstrated dramatic successes with teaching the diversity of students they have responsibility for educating.

The staff at VIDA learned, and continues to learn, how to better meet the needs of those they serve, and it's all because their principal believes in them. He has worked to create an environment where they feel valued and are empowered to do better for their students. This team has created a culture of learning that is not just about a shared purpose but is also truly owned and moved forward by everyone. As Shelley Burgess and Beth Houf share in their book, *Lead Like a PIRATE*, "People are less likely to tear down what they have helped to build."

Culture Is Everything in Schools

Nothing is more inspiring than working toward a common goal with people who share your passion and commitment. This collaboration creates a contagious vibe. Working with such a team motivates us to be better and makes us want to provide similar passion-filled experiences for others. In short, workplace culture impacts our behavior.

When schools or districts focus on compliance and mandates to implement programs and procedures, voice and choice are limited, which squashes creativity and innovation. On the flip side, an environment that honors the expertise of the educators can empower those in our schools who are working with the students every day and can help them make informed decisions based on the needs of the learners.

In many conversations about curriculum and instruction in schools, I still hear the focus on implementing programs with "fidelity" to cover the curriculum. At the district level, however, the vision is about developing critical and creative thinkers and problem solvers. If you have policies about fidelity and expect compliance in your classroom, school, or district, I challenge you to consider whether fidelity and compliance are really the goals.

Do you expect everyone to be on the same page at the same time? Or do you want to create authentic learning experiences? It's hard to do both. This doesn't mean that the standards and the curriculum are irrelevant. But rather than expecting the learner to adapt to the curriculum, allow the curriculum to meet the needs of the learner and use it in service of meaningful learning outcomes. Personal and authentic learning experiences require knowing the learners whom you serve.

We can change policies and implement new programs, but if we don't create school cultures where people feel valued and free to take risks in pursuit of learning and growth, we will miss out on our greatest opportunity to change how students learn. This mindset, which Dr. Chagala put front and center while envisioning VIDA, is absolutely foundational to shifting practices. To see the changes that we know are necessary in education, we must trust teachers—and they must trust themselves—to make decisions and design learning experiences in ways that meet the needs of those in their classrooms.

What Kind of Culture Have You Created?

How do you respond when you don't have all the answers? How often do we hold teachers or students back from doing great things and exploring their passions because we aren't sure of the outcomes or they don't fit into the plan? Often in school, when we focus on answers and dismiss learners' unique ideas, we squelch creativity. Instead, encouraging people to ask more questions, empathize with others, and seek problems to solve can kindle their creative spark.

Culture is made up of the collective attitudes, beliefs, and behaviors of the group, and everyone contributes to this. If we want to create learning experiences that unleash the talents that live in all students, teachers, and administrators, we have to push back against existing norms and traditions. We have to intentionally design a culture that serves the larger goals.

At the beginning of a meeting or on the first day of class, the leader commonly defines expectations and sets norms for how the group will work together. This is an important step in setting up the culture, but it's more important to attend to how people act. Is everyone's voice honored? Is the leader seeking correct answers only or encouraging questions?

The following factors are critical to the culture of learning and innovation at VIDA:

- An emphasis on relationships to meet the needs of the learners and align the school with the world in which students live.
- High expectations with support and inspiration from colleagues and administration.
- Autonomy to take risks and create amazing opportunities for learners.

Concluding Thoughts

Too often, I hear stories from educators who are frustrated by mandates, bureaucratic systems, and a lack of resources and support. You, too, might be frustrated with an ineffective system that moves uninspired and disconnected kids through school.

But education doesn't have to be this way! Dr. Chagala's leadership at VIDA highlights the reality that a school's culture, which everyone helps to create, contributes to how teachers see their roles and the impact they have on students. We all thrive when we feel valued and have positive relationships with colleagues at work. These relationships are also the most predictive of teachers' job satisfaction and intentions to stay in the teaching profession.

When you believe that relationships don't matter or that they will just happen, your culture suffers. The shift at VIDA didn't happen by chance. Dr. Chagala, an amazing educator and principal, worked with his team to create a culture, a shared way of doing things, that values people first and creates the conditions for everyone to learn, develop, and grow.

If you put learning, teaching, and leading to create opportunities for students above focusing on test scores or managing programs, you, too, can create the kind of environment in which people feel valued, cared for, and empowered to learn and make an impact. And the ultimate result is improved student outcomes.

Three Questions for Conversation

1. Does your culture support the type of learning that you value?
2. Does your culture value and promote growth and development for all learners?
3. How do you model what you expect of others?

MORE ABOUT DR. KATIE MARTIN

Dr. Katie Martin is the chief impact officer at the Learner-Centered Collaborative and author of *Learner-Centered Innovation and Evolving Education.* Katie has worked in diverse contexts to learn, research, and support deeper learning for all students. She has served as a middle school English language arts teacher and as an instructional coach, and led the district's new teacher mentoring program. She teaches in the Graduate School of Education at High Tech High and is on the board of Real World Scholars.

As a leader, educator, and changemaker, Katie's experience in research and practice guides her belief that if we want to change how students learn, we must change how educators learn. She aspires to do that by creating experiences that empower all learners to develop knowledge, skills, and mindsets to thrive in a changing world. As a mom, she wants her kids to have learning experiences in school that build on their strengths and interests, and she is passionate about making sure educators are equipped to do that for all kids. You can connect with Katie on social media at @KatieMartinEdu or on her website, KatieLMartin.com.

11

Construction Projects and a Few Meltdowns:

How Monique Taught Me to Learn and Lead

LAINIE ROWELL

Everyone has something to contribute to this world. It's just a matter of being given that opportunity to do so.

—Grace Hightower

I have been blessed with many excellent teachers. My first-grade teacher showed me love and kindness as I struggled through my parents' divorce. She was pregnant that year and named her daughter Lainie. Talk about going above and beyond! (Yeah, I know: she probably just liked the name. But I am going to pretend she was inspired by me.)

In sixth grade, I switched schools, and my teacher made sure I felt welcome and included even though I was surrounded by kids who had known one another since kindergarten. Even though I was far more interested in playing softball and doing competitive cheerleading than academics, I had teachers who noticed me and cared. So many teachers have positively influenced my life, and I appreciate them more than I could ever convey.

It's hard to imagine going into education without aspiring to impact the lives of those we lead in learning. It's a given, right? If we do our jobs, we might get an occasional slow clap as we walk into the classroom or a mention in the valedictorian's speech. Not quite.

This isn't *Dead Poets Society*, and most of us don't get an "O Captain! My Captain!" moment. More commonly, we'll get an email or message on social media from a student we taught years ago who wanted to tell us that what we did really mattered. We had an impact.

Considering how good it feels to be recognized for our work, you'd think we would constantly show appreciation for the administrators who have helped us reach greatness. After all, the work of great teachers is typically supported by an administrator who knows when to support and when to move out of the way. Yet far too often, administrators hear sentiments like, "That's why you get paid the big bucks"—another way of saying, "You are not deserving of our support and appreciation."

Education is a little like dominoes, with one action prompting another: an administrator positively impacts a teacher, who positively impacts countless students, who go on to change the world. Do we take the time to give these administrators the affirmations that they, like all of us, crave in some way?

Because of an Administrator

When George asked me to write this chapter about an administrator, I jumped at the chance. The idea of writing this felt like a public practice of deep reflection and gratitude. I felt joy just thinking about it. I could not wait to start.

Many leaders have had a huge influence on me. Don't worry, I won't break the rules and name more than one, though Steve Glyer, Mike Lawrence, Alan November, and Christine Olmstead deserve a mention. (That didn't count, did it?) Instead, I want to acknowledge the administrator who had faith in me first and who completely changed the trajectory of my career—and therefore my life.

Her name is Dr. Monique Huibregtse.

A Blessing in Disguise

In my third year as an educator, I was teaching first grade at a school I loved. This was an exceptional school. It had everything you could dream of as a teacher: strong leadership, collaborative staff, kiddos eager to learn, and supportive families. It wasn't the first school I taught at. I had worked hard to get there, knowing it was an environment where I would thrive.

When I landed a position there, I was ecstatic. Then came the catch: the district was opening a new school, so about half the students at my school would be moving to the new building the following year. As we know, fewer kids mean fewer teachers. Being a new teacher and understanding that last in usually meant first out, I saw the writing on the wall. I had two choices: be involuntarily transferred to another school in the district or apply for the new school. With very little hope of success, I opted for the latter.

I vividly remember walking into the portable that was serving as the temporary office. (The new school didn't even have a finished campus yet. It was literally exposed two-by-fours, A-frames, and dirt. More on that later.) My interview was with the new principal, Monique, who was also new to the district. It was nerve-racking. To this day, I'm not sure I've ever seen anyone look more polished and professional in person. Even the way she carried herself was extraordinary.

Don't get me wrong, she was as kind and as welcoming as could be. She was just so impressive, and it added to my anxiety. She asked me a series of standard interview questions. Then she asked the tech questions. Eeek! I was a total tech neophyte. I admitted as much, and then she asked the next question, which not only put me at ease, but also made me want to follow this leader to the new school. She said, "Are you willing to learn? We will all be learning together." I was in!

Great Leaders See Greatness in Others

Once we got together as a staff, I was blown away by the team she had assembled. It was a group of highly dedicated, hardworking, enormously talented educators who never stopped learning. I had no idea what I'd done to deserve this team, and the imposter syndrome set in quickly. Clearly, Monique saw things in me that I couldn't even imagine if she thought I belonged with this group.

Now, if you have never opened a brand-new school, let me tell you: it is an all-hands-on-deck kind of situation. It doesn't help when your new campus's construction is six months behind schedule and you start the new school year in portables on another campus till construction is finished.

There was so much work to do, and we were a small group: thirteen teachers, a principal, an office manager, and a part-time nurse. We worked together, in real time, to make the countless decisions that needed to be made. To this day, I don't know how Monique steered the ship, but she did it with such grace and patience. I can't recall her ever being flustered or frustrated—she just focused on doing right by the kids, her staff, and the community. It paid off.

We all worked really hard, not because we had to but because we wanted to. This was our school, and we were making it an amazing place to learn and thrive. We were driven by our purpose, clocking twelve-hour days regularly. And that was just the time we spent on campus. Most nights, we went home and worked some more. (This is when I first realized that having a laptop and being able to email 24-7 is both a blessing and a curse.) I wish I could tell you that, as a young teacher in my early twenties, I embraced the challenges and hard work with patience, an even temper, and incredible flexibility. But that was not me. At least, not all the time.

Grace, Patience, and Caring Advice

One particularly embarrassing moment in my career was when the superintendent came to visit us in our temporary location. Tensions were high. We had worn out our welcome on the shared campus. Construction on the new site kept getting delayed. Monique stayed positive and did everything humanly possible to keep our morale up, but I was beyond frustrated. The superintendent sat down with us to explain that rain and other factors beyond anyone's control would push moving to the new site back. Again. The original plan had been for us to be housed on the other campus for a few weeks, so we lived out of boxes, never sure when we would up and move.

So, when the superintendent arrived with promises of yet another move date, I let him have it. I was sarcastic and, I'm ashamed to say, outright rude. We couldn't trust the move dates, I told him, so why did he even bother predicting? I still cringe thinking about how I must have embarrassed Monique. I was acting like an entitled, petulant child.

At some point, I realized the confrontation was not going well, and I dreaded talking to Monique afterward. But as she did countless times, she offered me grace and patience. She said she understood how frustrating the not knowing is (something I struggle with to this day), and instead of scolding me and reminding me to be a decent human being, which I deserved, she offered me some advice. She told me that she saw great things in me, but that relationships are important, so it probably isn't a wise career move to offend the highest-ranking leader in the district. I was in awe of the fact that she wasn't even worried how my behavior reflected on her. Instead, she used it as a teachable moment for me.

I'd like to say that this was the last time my impatience and immaturity emerged, but it wasn't. I did, however, learn to take the long view and be respectful even when I disagreed with someone.

A Culture of Learning for Kids and Adults

We did eventually move to the new campus. The work didn't get easier, but it was so magical. We were no longer imposing on another site; we were home. And our new home was designed for innovation with technology. We didn't have a lot of tech, but what we did have was the latest and greatest, and I was excited to learn.

Monique encouraged all of us to do as much learning as possible, and she didn't stop there. She taught us to learn and share. When someone went to a conference, they'd present what they had learned at a staff meeting. She also arranged for classes to be covered so we could go into each other's classrooms to model, co-teach, and see each other in practice. She encouraged us to present at conferences and earn certifications. The culture of learning she cultivated was as nurturing for the adults as it was for the kids.

As the years went on, our school grew. We doubled in size within three years! And I really embraced being an adult learner and engaging in all the opportunities Monique provided. I even enjoyed learning beyond digital pedagogy, and I kinda nerded out on the technical side, too. Eventually, I became the go-to for tech issues. As George would say, "If it had a power button, they were coming to me." And this led to the next major meltdown I had.

Another Mistake, Another Opportunity to Learn

Even though I had taken on additional responsibilities by choice, I still stormed into Monique's office one day, ranting about how I couldn't possibly be expected to teach full-time, lead professional learning regularly, *and* provide tech support. Here I was again, entitled and petulant. And here she was again, graceful and patient. She said, "So, what is your proposal?"

I stared at her, completely confused. What was she asking me? *Why* was *she* asking *me*? She was the leader; she had all the answers.

"Lainie," she said, "when you have a problem, I need you to come with some ideas so we can work together on the best possible solution." There was a brilliance to the way she was framing the conversation. She wasn't telling me I was on my own. She was teaching me to be a problem solver, not just a squeaky wheel.

I went home with her words on my mind and thought about what I really needed in order to move forward and avoid burnout. I went in to Monique's office the next day with ideas, and we had a conversation. In the end, we came up with a plan that allowed me to stay in the class-room with my kiddos and also have a little release time to support the staff school-wide.

Win-win.

Lifting Others Up, Even When It Doesn't Serve Your Interests

A couple of years later, thanks to Monique's faith in my abilities and coaching of my skills, I was offered a district leadership position. I was thrilled at the opportunity to learn and lead in a different capacity, but it was hard to accept the position knowing how much time and effort she had invested in me. She had, of course, written a glowing letter of recommendation and knew I was potentially leaving, but I still dreaded telling her.

I walked into her office and gave her the news. She was so happy for me. Genuinely happy. She wasn't thinking about herself—the impact this would have on her team, the responsibilities she would need to get covered—but was proud and excited for me.

Impact through Actions

There are not enough words to express the profound effect Monique had on my life. She is a stellar example of a leader.

Throughout my career in education, so many people have supported me, challenged me, and given me opportunities. As I reflect, these are the common threads they shared:

- Focus on relationships first, establish trust, and build rapport
- Model underpromising and overdelivering
- Give others as much credit as possible, rather than take credit for themselves
- Have high expectations, provide opportunities for growth, and empower others to deliver on those expectations
- Lead with humility and don't let their egos, wants, or needs stand in the way of other people's success

To this day, Monique is still cheering me on. I recently emailed her to thank her for all she has done for me, and here was her response:

> I am always so proud of you. You have truly excelled in your journey in educational leadership. I am always so happy to be in meetings with you now, so many years later, seeing you in your many roles. Your passion for what you do is so evident and genuine. It is this energy that pulls others into your work. I love it!

I still have this message in my in-box. I keep it there to remind me of the impact one person can have on someone else's life. Monique, thank you for believing in me and putting me on an education leadership pathway! I love what I do, and I am doing it because of you.

The reality is, leaders don't always know when they've made a difference in someone's life because often it isn't about one monumental event. It's about consistently knowing when and how to support others to achieve their greatness.

Monique never once said this to me but constantly modeled it through her actions. She made me a better leader and teacher and set the standard of the support I want to provide others in my own work every day.

Three Questions for Conversation

1. We know that supporting our peers requires ongoing, job-embedded coaching. How do you (or can you) consistently support others to achieve their greatness?

2. How do you practice grace and patience with kids, peers, and families? Share specific examples.

3. How do you practice gratitude to give back to those who invest in you? Do you find value in publicly acknowledging others? Why or why not?

MORE ABOUT LAINIE ROWELL

Lainie Rowell is an educator and international consultant. She is dedicated to building learning communities, and her areas of focus include designing innovative learning experiences, online/blended learning, and professional learning. During her more than twenty years in education, Lainie has taught elementary, secondary, and higher education. She also served in a district-level leadership position supporting twenty-two thousand students and twelve hundred teachers at thirty-three schools.

As a consultant, Lainie's client list ranges from Fortune 100 companies like Apple and Google to school districts and independent schools. She is a TEDx speaker with more than fifteen years' experience presenting at local, regional, and international conferences. Since 2014, Lainie has been a consultant for the Orange County Department of Education's Institute for Leadership Development. She is the lead author of the book *Evolving Learner:*

Shifting from Professional Development to Professional Learning from Kids, Peers, and the World and cohost of the podcast *Lemonade Learning.* You can connect with Lainie on Instagram and Twitter at @LainieRowell or on her website, LainieRowell.com.

PART III

What Advice Would You Give to Your First-Year Teacher Self?

12

On Our Single Toughest Days, We Still Can Make a Lifetime of Difference

GEORGE COUROS

Each one of us can make a difference.
Together we make change.
—Barbara Mikulski

At the time, our mistakes can feel like the end of the world. But even in our worst moments as educators, we are often still positively influencing the lives of so many students. And that impact will last a lifetime.

The stories in this section will remind you of just that. They'll also remind you that a single mistake doesn't make you a bad teacher. Sometimes mess-ups help us grow. And, yes, we can always grow and improve in our careers. The moment you stop believing that statement, you should probably cease teaching because you are comfortable with stagnating.

I am always reminded of the importance of growth in the profession when I receive emails from teachers who have taught for thirty, forty, or fifty years and are trying something new to better themselves for their students. Those are actions that I am always inspired by.

Of course, even those superstars have had bad moments, bad days, and probably even some bad weeks. Ask longtime teachers, and most will point to moments in their teaching careers (some longer than others) that still embarrass them to this day.

For example, in my first year of teaching, I wanted to be the "cool" teacher. We had to teach poetry that year, and I remember thinking how I'd been much more interested in song lyrics than I was poetry as a student. (They're not exactly the same thing, but whatevs. I was going to be cool!). So instead of planning lessons on poetry, I had put together an awesome unit, asking students to research and discuss Canadian music lyrics.

The way I saw it, not only would this help bring awareness to some great musicians in our country, but the familiarity would bring a certain excitement to my students. In fact, at the beginning, my class loved the unit and thought it was really interesting to study the musicians who would eventually go on to inspire the next generation of Canadian artists. PS: You're welcome for Justin Bieber, Drake, and the Weeknd, and don't even get me started on how influential Celine Dion and Alanis Morissette are in the music world. That is a jagged little pill that will make your heart go on!

As the unit was coming to a close, I had taken my class to our school computer lab for a fun activity. Using our dial-up internet and Yahoo! search (this is 1999, people!), they were tasked with researching one of my favorite Canadian bands. Unfortunately, this band was named Barenaked Ladies.

So, as I am watching my students slowly hunt and peck the name "Barenaked Ladies" into the search bar, I thought, *"Wait a minute. They might not find the band!"* Thank goodness students were not fluent in their typing skills. For once in my life, I was so extremely grateful for slow internet.

We had a master power switch in the lab, and I quickly shut down all of the computers, told the students that the power went out, and we went back to the classroom, where we studied poetry for the rest of the unit.

Crisis averted, and job saved!

People Look Up to You Even in Your Worst Moments

To give the other authors space to share their stories, I won't list the multitude of things that I would change about my teaching were I given a chance to go back. But let's just look at the highlights: my lack of understanding of the curriculum, an archaic sense of what assessment is and could be, and the bad classroom management practices (like the sticker charts I used for behavior) that make me cringe to this day.

Believe me, the mistakes didn't end after my first year. Even as an administrator (and still to this day), I've flubbed interpersonal relationships by trying to fix people instead of helping them. My understanding of how important it is to make people feel valued and help them move forward is a place where I have grown significantly.

But one thing that I feel I got right from the beginning is my focus on relationships. Dr. David Pysyk, a principal who mentored me even without knowing it, said, "A teacher who is great with relationships and bad with curriculum will last a lot longer than one who is the opposite." He acknowledged that he preferred hiring someone who was good at both, but a relationship-builder was a close second. While he could help someone improve their pedagogical approach, he couldn't teach them to like kids. That has always resonated with me.

Many of my first-year (and current-year) mistakes were softened by my focus on building relationships with my students. I spent a great deal of time at recess playing basketball, skipping rope, or chatting with students. Getting to know kids on a personal level seemed to create room for me to make mistakes that would be easily forgiven. In fact, as a new principal, I made a lot of decisions that, looking back, I realize I should have handled differently. But I know that I was given leeway by my staff because they knew how much I cared about the students. And that is one thing, no matter my deficiencies, they knew they had in common with me.

And if you have any doubt that you matter to your students, just look at what happens when you run into kids outside the classroom. You may feel like students don't connect with you, especially if you work with older kids. But stumble upon students at a grocery store, and they'll act like you're one of the Kardashians. Oh, they might pretend like they don't care about—or even like—you, but as soon as they see you outside of school, they make the biggest deal.

It happened to me one Saturday when I was a principal. I was grocery shopping when I saw one of my students. He seemed five seconds from fainting. He said, "Mr. Couros! What are you doing here?"

"Um," I said. "Buying food?"

He couldn't believe it. We chatted for five to ten minutes and then said our goodbyes. He had the biggest smile on his face for the whole interaction.

The following Monday, I arrived at school about thirty minutes before it opened, and the same student was waiting outside the door for me. This was totally out of character. He came up to me and said, "Mr. Couros! I saw you at the grocery store!"

I said, "I know! I talked to you!"

I realized something then—he'd thought about that short interaction for the whole weekend. Even though I was still growing and trying to get better, he saw my heart and knew how much I cared, and that was what resonated.

You have that same power in your hands. Use it wisely and with love.

It Goes By Fast

In the next chapters, you are going to hear from some very accomplished educators, all of whom are well respected and admired (especially by me). They'll get vulnerable as they share the lessons they have learned in their teaching careers and how those lessons have helped shape them today. We all have these stories—if I shared all of mine, this would be a *War and Peace*-size book of mistakes.

What I will tell you from my experience is to appreciate and recognize the moment you are in right now, no matter where you are in your career. Even if you feel your career is full of flaws and screw-ups.

When I first started, I remember my colleagues sharing that the first twenty years of their careers went by in the blink of an eye. I looked at them and thought they were exaggerating, and twenty years later here I am. Where did the time go?

This will seem unrelated, so bear with me. When I was a kid, I asked for the exact same present each Christmas: a dog. And every year: no dog.

I swore that when I became an adult, I would get a dog. True to myself, I signed my first teaching contract, went straight to the SPCA, and adopted a few-years-old dog that I named Kobe. Kobe was not only the gift I always wanted, but he kind of signified a new chapter in my life, moving from being a student to a teacher. Kobe seemingly entered adulthood with me, and all of a sudden, I was responsible for something more than myself. I loved that dog, and through several moves and several jobs, Kobe (and, later, my other dog, Shaq) made the moves with me. Wherever I went, they were by my side.

Kobe had been with me when I started teaching, and eventually, he was there for my first days as a new principal. I'd lived alone for years, and he was my only constant. In the first few days of my second year as a principal, Kobe seemed a little ill so I took him to the vet to get checked. I still remember the veterinarian looking at me and saying, "I don't want to tell you what to do, but Kobe is in a lot of pain, and I don't think he should continue feeling this."

Kobe's presence in my life was significant. He was there at the beginning of adulthood, and his illness seemed like a test of how adult I had become. Could I do the right thing when it was the hardest thing to do? As tears streamed down my face, I asked the vet if I could have a few hours with Kobe before I put him down, and she said, "Of course. Do what you need."

What I needed was to give Kobe a great last memory, so I took him to McDonald's, bought him a cheeseburger and a McFlurry, and had those last moments with him. I took him to the veterinarian and petted him as he peacefully passed away.

As hard as this is to remember, it reminds me of the love I received from my school when I returned. When I was on my own. My closest family was seven hours away, and living on my own made dealing with the loss extremely hard.

But I was not alone. Teachers checked in on me. Students comforted me as I shared what had happened. Many saw me as a principal before, but now they all saw me as a human who just happened to be a principal. I am sure I could have made it through that time without that school community, but I am so grateful that I didn't have to. They were there for me when I needed it most.

That was my first brush with loss but not my last. Many colleagues and students have been my rocks when I needed them the most, and for some reason, those moments seem frozen in time.

Much of my career is a blur. I remember little moments, but it seems like everything has happened so fast. I spent a lot of my career moving from place to place, or to new positions. One of my regrets is that I spent so much time looking forward that I didn't spend enough time appreciating the present. The little moments that should be clear became blurs in my rearview mirror.

Feel free to look forward to where you want to be and what you want to do. But no matter where you are in your career or life, don't ignore the current moment. It might be great, or it might be hard, but it is a moment of significance if you treat it as such. Like the mistakes you'll read about in the upcoming chapters—such as my Barenaked Ladies moment—you will look back at those hard times fondly and with a laugh if you allow yourself to grow.

During the COVID-19 pandemic, I learned that there is a difference between being "home" and being "present." Being present is not just about where you are physically but also where you are mentally and emotionally at any particular time.

I'm reminded of a quote from the movie *My Dog Skip*. During my almost disastrous poetry unit, the class asked me to watch the movie with them because they knew how much I loved my dogs. In it, the narrator says: "Why, in childhood and youth, do we wish time to pass so quickly—we want to grow up so fast—yet as adults, we wish just the opposite?"

As you read the stories ahead and feel connected to the ups and downs of education, know that the best way to slow time in adulthood and in our careers is to appreciate the moment you are in—both the good and the bad. We can look forward to the future, but it doesn't mean we can't find opportunities to embrace the present moment. As the twenty-year veteran told me twenty years ago, it goes by fast.

—13—

Accept, Ask, Approach

STEPHANIE ROTHSTEIN

Asking for help is a power move. It's a sign of strength to ask and sign of strength to fight off judgment when other people raise their hands. It reflects a self-awareness that is an essential element in braving trust.
—Brené Brown

Accept

I began student teaching in the fall of 2003 at El Camino High School in South San Francisco, California, a neighborhood otherwise known as The Industrial City—no joke: the words are literally printed on a hill near the school. After observing and volunteering in the English and English Language Development (ELD) classes in the spring of 2003, I immediately felt at home. I even chaperoned an ELD field trip that one of my master teachers put together.

We took public transit (known to locals as BART) to San Francisco, easy enough since the school was located across from the South San Francisco BART station. We rode the cable car, went to Fisherman's Wharf, and ate together. I felt lucky to support these incredible students as they held conversations, used maps, and navigated public transportation. Seeing their faces light up as they hopped onto the cable car, ate a hot dog they purchased from a street vendor, or walked near the water, taking in all the smells of San Francisco, I knew I had found what I was meant to do and where I was meant to do it. (I won't mention the part about losing two students; don't worry, they were just fine. But if you are ever on a field trip, remember to gather student phone numbers just in case.)

My final student teaching semester flew by with the support of my master teachers, Raven Coit and Derek Padilla. I called them my mom and dad, and they really did take care of me at the school. They sympathized when I had to observe a teacher who had a tendency to dim my light, brought me to sporting events, included me in middle-of-the-night spirit week decorating, and sent me down the hall to make all of the copies because, "You need to make friends with the amazing people in the copy room and front office."

They also became real friends, rooting for me as I began job hunting that December. I was resolved to wait a semester and finish my master's degree, while substitute teaching in the meantime. In December, I learned that the teacher across the hall was quitting. She walked out of the school and stopped teaching altogether. The principal asked whether any of the English subject student teachers wanted to interview for the position. It sounded pretty great to me.

I was hired to start right after winter break, in January 2004. I had two weeks to figure out what I was doing. I had taught ninth- and eleventh-grade English as a student teacher, but I would now teach English to tenth and twelfth graders. To top it all off, their teacher had left them in the middle of the school year, so they believed they were the reason she left.

My first-period class was twelfth-grade English, so most of the students were seventeen or eighteen years old. I was only a few years older and tried my very best to appear as mature as possible, wearing glasses, putting my hair in a bun, and wearing a really uncomfortable suit. I greeted that first class near the door, most of them towering over my five-foot-three frame. Most of them came in wearing basketball uniforms. Some even held basketballs, seemingly ready to throw them across the classroom if things got a little boring.

I wrote Ms. Lipman (my maiden name) on the board, erased it, and wrote it again. This was it.

My first day in *my* classroom.

It didn't matter that there were still posters from the previous teacher on the wall and shelves full of books she'd picked through before she left. I could get to that later. At the moment, I was busy with my first ever class as a real teacher.

The warning bell rang, and in came Ron, the campus security guard. He took one look at me and said, "Um, miss, you need to sit down with the rest of your class and wait for your teacher to arrive."

Clearly, trying to look older was not working on anyone. "I am the teacher," I said. "I was just hired to take over."

Ron was not amused. Or trusting. "Very funny. Have a seat."

I literally had to walk over to my desk and show him my teacher ID. I am sure I turned bright red, mortified that *this* was my introduction to the students. But something unexpectedly wonderful came of that moment.

I thought the students would laugh at me, but instead one student defended me. One of the basketball players said, "Yeah, our other teacher left. She's new. She used to be across the hall." He didn't have to do that, but I felt like it opened a door. (Note to self: Make sure you know any campus security staff before your first day!)

While that moment was awkward, it also helped me laugh at myself and breathe. I was anxious. I wanted this to go right. But really, is there a right? There was no way, in the two weeks I had to prepare myself to start, that I could have planned for everything. I couldn't track down campus security when I was struggling to prepare all of the students' lessons. I didn't even know their names!

I paused in my very stiff suit and just laughed, really laughed out loud. The students started laughing, too. "Well, that was a perfect intro," I said. "I didn't even pay him to do that. I'm Ms. Lipman."

I laid my mapped-out lesson plans on my desk and didn't use them. I went around the classroom, and students told me their names and shared something with me and the class they felt comfortable sharing aloud. Some chose to give me advice or tell me embarrassing moments they had from when they were ninth graders. "When you get to fifth period," one student said, "make sure you tell my brother that if he is mean to you, we'll have a talk."

I learned that there really isn't anything that will make me fully prepared. I was like the students navigating San Francisco for the first time. I encountered moments I had not planned for. But that is real life, and that is what it means to work with people.

I wish I could go back and tell my younger self that I needed to stop comparing my readiness to that of others. Other teachers had curriculum binders and knew what they were teaching. They had it all together, and here I was being mistaken for a student on my first day. What I wouldn't give to go back and tell 2004-era Stephanie that none of that actually matters. None of that angst was my actual job. My actual job was helping us all grow as people, and I needed to accept that in order to focus on the people sitting in front of me. Laughing with them helped me do that.

Sure, it wasn't how I saw my introduction going. And it might've been embarrassing for a moment. But it taught me that I need to stay present, be myself, and take the job as it comes.

Ask

I feel like I have had multiple first-year moments. I will never forget my first day on the Los Gatos High School campus. I went in to set up my classroom. I was nervous, once again. Even though I had six years of teaching under my belt, I was the person with the least experience at this school.

I was dressed like I was going to teach, even though I was there to set up my classroom. I wanted to make a good impression. I walked into the main office—remember, I had learned to talk to the front office staff—and asked if they had a cart I could borrow. They wheeled one out to me. I loaded it up with books and supplies that I'd brought from my time at El Camino.

As I pushed the heavy cart up the ramp to my second-floor classroom, I made it three steps before the cart rolled back at me. There I was in heels, marching up the ramp and sliding back down, covered in sweat and feeling completely alone. I didn't want anyone to see me as weak or think I didn't know what I was doing. Of course, that's not the only reason I didn't stop. At that point, if I had let go of the cart, it would've rolled over me and taken out anyone in its path. I had to keep going.

I took off my shoes and added them to the cart, but it didn't help! I had on panty hose (who wears panty hose?) so I struggled to gain traction. So, there I was, shoeless and trapped in the middle of the ramp, with my back against the cart to keep from dying. That's when I found scissors in my cart of supplies. I cut the feet off the panty hose and started to get a grip on that freshly waxed ramp. After what felt like hours, I made it to the top and into my classroom. When I got to my room, I quickly opened the door, pushed the cart inside, closed the door, and cried.

That climb up the ramp had decimated my confidence. I figured everyone would know that I wasn't good enough to be at this school. I couldn't even move my supplies into my classroom.

It wasn't until I'd been there for months that I felt comfortable enough with the staff to share this story. I first told the teacher across the hall, Sharon Smith, who said, "You know that there are people who will help you move your supplies into your classroom. You just have to fill out a request form and ask."

What? I just have to ask? Yes, my awkward encounter with the ramp could have easily been avoided if I had just asked for help. I was so scared to let others know that I didn't know what I was doing that I didn't ask for help. I assumed they would judge me. But I was making life so much harder for myself.

Seeking out support and help is so important. We shouldn't be struggling alone. As the chair of a design thinking pathway, I know that collaboration is key. If I could go back, I would tell myself to model this for my students. After all, I ask them to collaborate every single day.

I will never forget one student, Ava, who told me that she specifically applied for our pathway because "collaboration is hard for me, and I want to push myself and try to grow." When she first began, I could see that she was trying, but it was really hard for her to listen openly and hear anyone else's ideas. She would talk over anyone who had a differing opinion and dominate the conversation. And the truth is, when I didn't ask for help, I was doing the exact same thing. I was dominating my own internal conversation. It may have been worse because I wasn't even willing to have the conversation.

If I'd had that conversation, I'd have saved myself the heartache and loneliness by tapping my first-year self on the shoulder and telling her to find people to challenge her and propel her forward. I would tell myself to be open, to listen, and to be willing to share.

I am lucky to have a support system now. I sit with these colleagues to work though project ideas, new readings, cross-curricular units, and technology tools. They are true thought partners and ask the tough but necessary questions. Some of them are people in my design thinking pathway; I have found others through conferences and social media. I no longer need to push that heavy cart of ideas up a steep and freshly waxed ramp alone.

Approach

Everyone who knows me knows that if music is on, I will be the first one out on the dance floor. That's just me. I am not an extrovert, but music moves me, and I love to be moved by it. I've started to think about the school year like a dance. The music, rhythm, and tempo might change, but there is always music playing. I just need to listen to it, understand which song is playing, and seek out the right dance for each moment. The hardest part of that first year of teaching is understanding the playlist and knowing which song is playing each day.

As February 2021 began, I found myself supporting my student teacher with an onslaught of emails. It was a difficult year teaching using a model that included virtual lessons, then hybrid, and finally ended with in-person teaching. There seemed to be an uptick in all of the messages: students having difficulty completing assignments, students needing more support, students sharing emotional turmoil, and students feeling stress. I could tell right away that this was weighing heavily on my student teacher, Stephanie Todd.

Seeing the classroom through her eyes has helped me remember the feelings of that first year. So, I shared with her something I wish I'd known my very first year of teaching: "There is an ebb and flow to the school year. Every year, February and March are tough. There's no way to sugarcoat this. They just are. Students feel it and so do educators."

I could see that she was internalizing these challenges in the exact way I had during my first year of teaching. In February and March, sports teams' seasons overlap with tryouts, we're preparing for testing, there's practice for the school musical, students are running in school elections, college acceptance notifications arrive, and the pace of the school year starts to pick up. It becomes a time when everyone is looking at the calendar and living for the next break. I advised my student teacher to approach this time with some grace for herself and for the students.

I wish I'd understood, back when I first started, that when you hit February, the playlist switches to "Say Something" by A Great Big

World and Christina Aguilera, a fairly mellow song with an undertone of sadness and feeling defeated, and plays on loop through March. Think deeply about the pace of each day and the dance you are asking of yourself and your students. While this is true for all times of the year, it is especially true for February and March. Preparing ourselves for that next song is key.

When I think back to where I began and who I am now, I realize a lot has happened over the eighteen years of my career so far. And that's a good thing. When I was in my first year of teaching, I never dreamed that one day I would be giving a talk that went on TEDx, writing articles for *Edutopia*, flying to Singapore for Google Innovator, meeting George Couros and being on his podcast, or even writing a chapter in this book. I don't think knowing any of this ahead of time would actually have changed me, though I might have been more nervous.

But there is a benefit to hindsight. There is a benefit to knowing the songs that are going to be played, to understanding my rhythm, and approaching the school year knowing some things are always constant. Because, after all, so many things are not.

I wish I'd known, as a first-year teacher, to ultimately accept myself, laugh, and take life as it comes. I wish I'd known that asking for help shows vulnerability and strength and leads to connections. I wish I'd known to emotionally prepare my approach by listening to the ebb and flow of a school year. Knowing these things will not stop you from experiencing challenges, but they will help you navigate and grow, which ultimately should be our goal for ourselves and our students.

Three Questions for Conversation

1. How did you deal with nervousness or anxiety at the start of your job or school year? What advice would you give other educators on how to best cope when entering new situations?

2. Asking for help is a sign of strength, not weakness. What are some strategies you have to reach out to others when you are struggling or need support?

3. We often give grace to others, but not ourselves. If you were to take the advice you would provide to others who were struggling in their careers, what would you share?

MORE ABOUT STEPHANIE ROTHSTEIN

Stephanie Rothstein is an educational leader focused on making education more collaborative and less competitive. She advocates for modeling the risks we expect of our students, which she shared in her TEDx Talk, "My Year of Yes to Me," published on ted.com. In her eighteen-plus years in education, Stephanie has taught English to grades nine through twelve, run the yearbook and AVID, and chaired the LEAD Design Thinking Pathway at Los Gatos High School for ten years. She is currently a teacher on special assignment and administrator in Northern California. Her continuous love of learning led her to become a Google Innovator, trainer, and coach, as well as to earn her administrative services credential. She is a cofounder of Global GEG, the creator of CanWeTalkEDU, and the author of numerous articles published on *Edutopia* and her own blog. She speaks at educational conferences around the world and was named CUE's 2021 Teacher of the Year. You can connect with Stephanie on Twitter at @stephedtech or through her website, stephedtech.com.

14

Leading and Learning with HEART

LIVIA CHAN

Authenticity is the language of visionaries.
—Andrena Sawyer

Think back to your very first year of teaching. What is the first word you think of? For me, it's *heartwarming*.

So many fond memories still warm my heart. It was one of the most unforgettable years in my two decades as an educator because of varied emotions and novel experiences. I experienced the highest highs and the lowest lows, self-doubt and self-determination. Most important, I treasured the relationships I built with six- and seven-year-olds, my first-year guinea pigs.

I used to regret my first year of teaching, comparing that inexperienced girl to the experienced woman she grew into. But I learned about self-compassion and how to honor my journey. I found encouragement and inspiration in the words of Maya Angelou, who said,

"People will forget what you said, people will forget what you did, but people will never forget how you made them feel."

I could have been better at teaching all of the subjects had I known then what I know now, but growth takes time. I may not have taught in the most effective way, but I did the best I could with the skills and knowledge I had at that time. No matter my mistakes, I poured myself into my students that year. And, without a doubt, they felt loved, cared for, and valued.

Everyone, regardless of profession, has a story to share about their first year in a new role. There's something special to tell because that year is full of first-time events, experiences, emotions, and relationships. First times can evoke a range of feelings, from the joy of a big win to fear of the unknown.

And there are *a lot* of unknowns during that first year. But the one thing we do know is ourselves. Be genuinely *you.*

When I think about who I am as an educator, I'm reminded of my goal to be authentic, kind, grateful, and positive. I love to have fun, build relationships, connect, show appreciation, commit to my daily best, and lead with my heart.

What about you? What are your key words? Record them. Post them where you can see them, and let them guide and remind you. This will help you grow through adversity.

> "We do not learn from experience . . . we learn from reflecting on experience."
>
> —John Dewey

So, what have I learned since my first year of teaching? A lot! I've grown professionally and personally, picking up nuggets of wisdom along the way. (Like the lesson I learned the day I invited a bunch of stuffed animals to assembly.)

Here are a few reflections I wish I could pass on to my first-year self. Hopefully you'll benefit from the knowledge I earned through making mistakes.

Have Fun and Don't Sweat the Small Stuff

I enjoy adding an element of fun or novelty to each day. When kids are having fun, they are happier, and learning tasks are more effective and memorable. Joyful students are more likely to put their hearts into learning, too. As a side effect, though, there's greater potential for the unexpected. And sometimes things go sideways.

So, I've learned to not sweat the small stuff and to embrace the outcome as part of learning. Of course, I hadn't mastered that skill in my first year as an educator.

I was teaching second- and third-grade students. In the first week, I asked them to bring in their favorite stuffed animal. They'd serve as comfort toys and a way to get to know one another better. This ended up being a daily and yearlong habit. Our little buddies came to lessons on the carpet, sat on desks as we worked, and simply kept us company. They added more fun and happiness—it was like having extra students in our community. My students absolutely loved it!

We were so used to bringing our stuffed animals everywhere that I forgot to tell my students to leave them behind for our first assembly in the gym. That was a mistake! Some of the kids were noticeably playing with them, bouncing them on their laps, and distracting themselves and others. I bet you can imagine what that might have looked like.

I noticed judgmental looks and felt so unsure of how best to proceed. I wanted to hide and just wished someone would help me fix the problem. I'm surprised that I still remember this seemingly insignificant moment, but I suppose that's what happens when a memory has such a strong emotional connection. In hindsight, I should have quickly collected our stuffed friends, but I was too afraid to stand out. The assembly felt like an eternity!

I was so embarrassed, and it bothered me all weekend. I was fearful of being judged and anticipated a stern talking-to when I returned to school on Monday. But nothing happened. In the grand scheme of things, this was not a big deal. First-year teachers make mistakes.

So don't be afraid to try new things. When faced with unintended consequences, let mistakes go. Put it into perspective, and don't sweat the small stuff. Have fun with all of your heart.

Every Interaction Is an Opportunity to Build Relationships

Relationships are built on a collection of interactions, each of which provides an opportunity to uplift others with our empathy, kindness, and gratitude. Our words and actions can make someone's day a brighter one. Over time, these positive interactions accumulate, strengthening our relationships.

Make each one count! Our relationships with students help build trust. And when students trust us, we can leverage our connection to more effectively influence overall growth and learning.

I strive to make our school year as memorable as possible. As George would say, make their second-grade year the best second-grade year they will ever have. I'm reminded again of Maya Angelou's statement that "people will never forget how you made them feel." By using every interaction to build meaningful relationships, they will remember feeling loved, cared for, and valued.

As a first-year teacher, I honestly had no idea that the things I did and the relationships I built would be memorable years later. I did not even think about the impact I could or would have on the lives of the children I taught. I lived in the here and now, enjoying the moments, teaching the lessons, and making it through the day. Now that I know my words and actions have the potential to last decades—possibly a lifetime—I see each person as a gift. Our relationship is also a gift. One that needs to be cultivated, treasured, and treated with value through every positive interaction.

These gifts give educators their superpower, and one that not all professions have. Each person, and the relationship we form with them, gives us the power to make a difference. Many people have stories about the teachers who cared deeply or changed the trajectory of their lives.

Not every teacher will have a life-changing effect on every student. The difference a teacher makes can vary based on the teacher and the student, and that's OK. But all teachers impact their students, so it's up to you make sure the difference you make is a positive one.

I try to apply the Peter Parker principle to teaching. He understood, when he became Spider-Man, that "with great power comes great responsibility."

I recently came to understand that our impact as educators is more of a responsibility. We have the power to raise a child up to new levels with words of affirmation but also very quickly tear down with the opposite. This power cannot be taken lightly. In every single word I say, in every single thing I do, and in every single activity I plan for the day, there is a purpose. There is an intention to it all. There has to be. After all, it is my responsibility to make our time together valuable, using those moments to build relationships, help my students grow, and impact their lives.

So, I daresay it is not the lessons in the curriculum that make a difference or change lives. It's our relationships. Through our connections with students, we can help them discover their passions, make an impact in their learning and growth, and help them realize they can go beyond their potential. Believe in them until they believe in themselves. That is what changes their life's trajectory.

The personal connection is what students remember years later, long after memories of your lessons have faded. It's why I'm still in touch with a woman I taught decades ago.

In my first year of teaching, I absolutely loved to write happy notes to my students. There were a few who especially enjoyed exchanging notes all year. Jaclyn, now twenty-nine years old, was one student who loved to write. To this day, we still keep in touch.

We recently exchanged pictures of our stuffed animals, Puppynose and Bubba. These little guys used to come with us to school every day. They have aged just like we have!

As she was going through her memory boxes, Jaclyn came across my notes. She had held on to these for a reason: they reminded her of our time together. She recently wrote, "You're always the first teacher who comes to my mind who made the biggest impact."

Wow. At the time, how was I to know those notes would make a difference? Even small gestures like this can help us build relationships and can go a long way toward impacting a child's life.

No matter where you are in your career, know your potential to make an impact. Do your best to make every single interaction count. There is always more than one way to say the same thing. What you say can either uplift or tear down. There is no in-between. Choose your words and actions with the purposeful intention to build strong relationships with others. Give of your heart.

Appreciation Fosters Relationships

One way to build relationships is by developing a practice of heartfelt gratitude. When I see students, the time I spend with them, and the relationships we form as gifts, I naturally feel more grateful. I thank students for many things over the course of the day, like making me smile, giving me the gift of attention, and working to their full potential. These interactions foster happiness and make them feel valued.

I encourage gratitude every day. After partner or collaborative group work, for example, I remind them to thank each other. Teaching, modeling, and encouraging thankfulness are powerful tools that you can use to build an appreciative classroom community. When students begin to see each other, their experiences, and even social difficulties through a lens of gratitude, it improves their relationships. Gratitude leads to greater happiness, well-being, and optimism, and it promotes a positive mindset. All of these qualities are necessary for building a caring environment for learning together.

One of the strategies I use in my work is to connect our hearts in Community Circle. This special community time is such a positive way to share inspiration and build our community as we listen and learn more about each other. It's my favorite daily routine! As one student wrote, "During Community Circle, I really love hearing what Ms. Chan is going to share with us."

Every week, we celebrate Thankful Thursday, when we take turns sharing feelings and what we are grateful for. It's wonderful to hear how grateful they are to come to school to be with friends, for fun learning, and for the kindness they see in our class. These heartwarming expressions of gratitude build relationships, make students feel valued, and definitely add happiness to our day.

See the world around you as a gift, and you'll find yourself happier and more grateful. Give appreciation often, and have students share in order to build a stronger community and culture of gratefulness. Lead with gratitude in your heart.

Reach Out

Teaching can be a lonely job if you let it. Unlike other professions, it requires true dedication to cultivate your own philosophy as you listen and learn. But you're selling yourself short if you go it alone. The path you follow allows you to improve with more time, practice, and mentoring. If you are fortunate, you'll have experienced teachers who will reach out, take you under their wings, and provide opportunities for mentoring.

In my first year, I was blessed with a friend named Anna. She regularly checked on me to see how I was doing and if I needed support. I've had such appreciation for Anna through the years, and the connection we continue to share never fails to bring me joy and gratitude. I still treasure how much she meant to me. I fondly remember how she made me feel: valued and well supported because of her gift of time and love.

If you don't have someone like Anna, then it's up to you to initiate. Find someone who teaches the same grade level, someone you are drawn to, or someone you feel some connection to. Find someone you believe will guide and uplift you. We are stronger and better together.

Since the pandemic, I made a life-changing discovery. I became a connected educator and experienced the true impact of having people I can lean on and learn from on a daily basis. I am so grateful that support is at my fingertips. With a tweet, text, phone call, or Zoom meeting, I can check in with people from around the world.

I never knew how valuable it was to have a personal learning network (PLN) beyond my school and district. I have grown more in the past ten months than I had in the past decade. And it's all because of the professional development I've had and relationships I've formed with people on Twitter and those who are part of the Teach Better Team.

Through these connections, I was gifted with numerous opportunities. I have grown personally and professionally, increased my confidence, found my voice, discovered my message, and learned to dream bigger than ever. I now feel joyfully alive every day and live a life full of purpose. Prior to the pandemic, I didn't know I needed a PLN, but now that I have one, I am sure I do not want to live without one. These deep relationships (all without meeting in person!) are so treasured. I am deeply grateful for every friendship I've made. We make each other better.

Make the most of the ability to connect with educators across the world—it's an advantage I wish I'd had when I first started! So, jump on whichever social media platform best suits you and start following people. Go ahead and lurk for a bit (yes, it is acceptable!), then start to actively participate in communities like weekly Twitter chats or Facebook groups. Reach out privately via direct message to people with whom you made a connection.

All it takes to find a community of like-minded educators is some courage and a desire to reach out. You will find a wonderful world of friendships waiting for you. As educators, we are truly better together, and that connection can expand across the globe if you choose to take advantage. Reach out with your heart.

Today's Best

I recently learned the "today's best" concept from Rae Hughart, CMO of the Teach Better Team, and it truly resonated.

Since the beginning of the year, I've been using Hans Appel's House Rules in my classroom. They're from his book, *Award Winning Culture*. I may not refer to them as our classroom's house rules, but I do let three essential questions guide us daily:

Will you do the right thing? (Character)

Will you do your very best? (Excellence)

What will you do in service to others today? (Community)

I made one small change to that second question, asking will you do *today's best*? This concept honors our varying thoughts and feelings from one day to the next and prompts us to give our best by using what we have in our hearts at that moment in time. The concept of today's best resonates with my students. It helps define what our best looks like, depending on the kind of day we are experiencing.

One morning, our beloved guinea pig, Coconut, passed away. Anyone who has ever lost a pet they loved knows that kind of deep pain. During our daily Community Circle, I told my students how much my heart hurt and how it had been a long time since my heart was in that much pain. I shared that I felt grateful for the six years we enjoyed Coconut's company and thankful it had been a long time since I felt such hurt. Oh boy, that was difficult to say without tearing up or giving in to the rawness of my heart, but I forged on.

I told them that I had considered staying home that day, but knew that my school family would raise my spirits and my soul would be filled by their smiles. Simply put, I needed them more than they needed me that day. I pledged that I would give them today's best. It was not going to look like yesterday's best, but that would be OK. I promised to give them all I had to give that day. My students filled my soul with their love, just as I knew they would.

If I could go back in time, I would meet myself on one of my more challenging days. I'd tell her what I'm telling all of you now—you are doing the best you can with the skills and knowledge you have. Acknowledge and celebrate your ongoing growth and small daily wins. Honor where you are. Don't compare yourself to others. If you gave it today's best, then no one can ask for anything more. If you didn't, acknowledge it and aim to do better the next day. Tomorrow is just another day to strive for "today's best." Accept what your heart has to give.

HEART

Everything I do, I do with my heart. I think and feel with my heart. I speak and act with my heart. I teach and lead with my heart. What does this mean? What is it that's in my heart? Genuine kindness, love, gratitude, positivity, and servitude. My heart is a gift to the communities I serve.

All teachers are leaders, even in their first year. You lead people in your community. You have a voice and so much to give to others. Aim to lead with heart—and HEART:

> **H**ave fun.
> Make **E**very interaction count as you build relationships.
> Have a heart full of **A**ppreciation.
> **R**each out, for we are stronger and better together.
> Aim for **T**oday's best.

Whether you are in your first year of teaching or have hit your fifty-year teaching anniversary, you can't go wrong if you lead with your heart. Be authentic. Be you!

Do these things, and you'll inspire students today to make a difference in the world tomorrow.

Three Questions for Conversation

1. In what ways did your students impact you during your first year?
2. Think back to your own first year as an educator. What was one relationship and/or interaction that brought encouragement and support through the unknown?
3. How do you lead with your heart? How do you inspire others to lead with theirs?

MORE ABOUT LIVIA CHAN

Livia Chan is an author and educator passionate about community, teaching, coaching, leading with her heart, and life-long learning. She truly believes in the power of connection and thoroughly enjoys building relationships by reaching out to uplift others with kindness and gratitude. For over twenty years, Livia has continued to experience the joy of teaching in the Greater Vancouver area in British Columbia, Canada, and loves her current role as a head teacher and classroom teacher. She is also honored to be a member of the Teach Better Team. Previously, Livia served on the district staff development team in learning technologies supporting K–12 educators. She would love to connect with you on Twitter and other social media platforms (she's @LiviaChanL) or on her blog, livchan.com.

15

Finding Ourself in the Pursuit of Improving Our Well-Being

EVAN WHITEHEAD

As we inhale soothing well-being through the radiant glow of an unsuspected lighthouse in the dark stormy nights of our life, we can come to feel the exhilarating rhythm of our heartbeat, finding compassion with ourselves and at one time reaching out to all the others.
—Erik Pevernagie

As I write this chapter, I am starting my twenty-third year in education. My career has spanned three decades, taking me from the classroom to the central office—for eleven of those years—where I served either as an assistant superintendent or a director.

There are certainly things I'd change about my time in all areas of education. But I'd most like to hit Rewind and give some advice to my younger self, who as a first-year teacher could've used it in order to avoid extreme stress and burnout.

In my opinion, education is the best profession in the world. As educators, we have the opportunity to shape and model the future of our society. But how many times have you heard a noneducator say something like, "Well, of course, it's the best profession in the world—you have the entire summer off!"

SMH!

Those outside of our profession are unable to see the invisible work that goes on every day. The idea that teaching is easy because we have summers "off" and paid holidays doesn't really tell the story of a day in the life of an educator. And it doesn't take into consideration the invisible backpacks educators carry.

It is my belief that there is one theme, an unspoken truth, that exists behind the scenes in the field of education: the "invisible back-pack." The term is rooted in the work of childhood trauma and Adverse Childhood Experiences (ACEs). It refers to all life experiences (positive and negative) that occur in and out of the classroom. Children carry these experiences with them when they come to school. However, the term is applicable to both children/students and adults/educators.

In *Emotional Poverty in All Demographics: How to Reduce Anger, Anxiety, and Violence in the Classroom*, Ruby K. Payne, PhD, discusses "emotional noise" in the classroom and the "emotional classroom dance." She asks the question, "What influences the emotional noise in the classroom?"

Consider the spaces of your school or organization. Can you visualize moments in which you have observed adults contributing as much to the emotional noise in a classroom as the students? Consider your own context. Can you still feel the tension of moments when people in your life came into your head while you were teaching? Does the stress of certain emotional triggers sometimes seep into your interactions?

Social-emotional well-being in the form of educator self-care is critical now more than ever. Our world has been turned upside down. What we once knew, and the consistency we once counted on, no longer exists. As a global pandemic, COVID-19 forced everyone to pause.

The irony is that although it's not how we wanted it, what has taken place was exactly what we have asked for: more time with our families, more hours in the day to start a new hobby (or pick up an old one), opportunities to focus on our health and physical fitness, or a chance to begin that novel we have always wanted to write. Often, the greatest discoveries are made out of necessity. Although some of the events of the past year could be categorized as traumatic and may have caused us to operate in crisis mode, we were all faced with two options: survive or thrive.

There are two things that create challenges to the overall mental health and well-being of educators today: a martyr complex and imposter syndrome. When combined, these can create increased levels of stress, angst, and educator burnout.

The Martyr Complex

Have you ever felt the need to do everything for everyone, consistently putting the needs of others before your own? Have you ever felt physically, mentally, or emotionally drained as an educator but pushed through anyway, putting your own mental and emotional health at risk? What is the excuse you use for pushing through?

Maybe you tell yourself, "My students need me." Or you rationalize, "If I don't do it, who else will?" Perhaps you tell yourself, "If I can save just one student or help one family, I will feel I have done my job and then I can take care of myself," or "As a leader, I have to set an example, and if I call in sick to work, how will that appear?" Early on, you might repeat an all-too-common excuse: "I have to make a good impression as a first-year teacher."

If you have asked yourself any of these questions or made any of these statements, you are not alone. I made these statements all the time, publicly and privately. It provided an excuse not to take care of myself and helped me tell a story that allowed me to rationalize what I was doing. It was like a free pass to avoid prioritizing my own health and well-being. This is an example of the martyr complex.

When we have a martyr complex, we often blame other people or situations for the challenges we have in our personal or professional lives. Traditionally, a martyr is someone who is willing to die for something they believe in. Within the context of the education profession, the martyr refers to someone who constantly puts the needs of others before their own, even to the detriment of their physical, mental, and emotional well-being.

So why is the martyr complex so dangerous within our profession?

Educators are often fixers, givers, and helpers by nature, which means they already put the needs of others before their own. But they also deal with complexities that have increased environmental stressors, such as poverty, crime, understaffed schools and districts, and high-need populations such as special education, English learners, Title I (low-income families), and McKinney-Vento homeless students, all of whom need tremendous support systems. When martyrs are working in these high-stress educational environments, they are more susceptible to burnout.

Unfortunately, I fell into this trap on my own education journey.

I started my career as a crisis interventionist at a therapeutic day high school. I worked as a teacher's assistant in self-contained special education classes. After encouragement from the lead teachers I was working with, I decided to go back to school and pursue a degree in special education. I took on a concentration in bilingual-bicultural special education and English as a second language, including a minor in Spanish language and literature.

My first full-time teaching job was in a self-contained special education high school program for students diagnosed with behavioral disorders and emotional disability. Looking back, I took on a lot of coursework over a short amount of time.

Later, I went on to work for the high school district in my community as a special education teacher and coordinator of the Latino Parent Outreach Program. I was quickly promoted to a dean of student discipline and, eventually, a community outreach and engagement coordinator working with Title I students as well as African American and Latinx students and their families. I created a student mentoring and college and career readiness program. During my tenure in that role, I cofounded the school gospel choir and started the first Black History Month program in the county. Even as I write this, I realize I took on too many responsibilities at once. Unfortunately, I am not the exception but the norm for far too many educators, no matter where they are in their career. We far too often say "yes" to everything possible, while saying "no" to ourselves.

You want proof? Stop for a second and reflect or even write down *all* of the things that you do that go beyond your job and what you expected your role to be. We can be passionate about our work in education—and we should be—but not to the point where we are so giving to others that we lose ourselves.

As the saying goes, we cannot fill others from an empty cup. We can only truly take care of others when we take care of ourselves.

Imposter Syndrome

Even though I felt I didn't have much in my own tank, at the encouragement of my administration I decided to pursue my master's degree in educational leadership and administration. I was already feeling overwhelmed with the responsibilities of working full-time, and my wife was expecting our second child and was the main caretaker of our two-year-old daughter. I completed my master's degree the same year I was awarded tenure in the district where I was working. Unfortunately, the district had just hired four assistant principals for the upcoming year. I am thankful for their transparency in telling me there wouldn't be any immediate administrative positions open and for their willingness to support me in my pursuit of administrative positions in other districts. In reflection, this was a turning point that would magnify my martyr complex and make visible my imposter syndrome.

Have you ever suffered from imposter syndrome? I sure have. Those days, I often felt like I did not belong with colleagues or supervisors who I thought were more intelligent, better equipped for the work, or in possession of attributes of success I thought I lacked.

Dr. Valerie Young shares the idea of the Superwoman/man falling into one of the subgroups of imposter syndrome and discusses how feeling inadequate is a hallmark trait as we overexert ourselves to "measure up" in our own minds. This can cause harm to a person's mental health and relationships with others. I exhibited the characteristics of the "Superman" when I made a habit of staying late at the office to prove I was "going above and beyond." I succumbed to external cultural expectations that said I, an African American, had to be twice as good to receive an opportunity. I was constantly seeking external validation from wherever and whomever provided it in order to fuel my internal self-worth.

When I began my administrative job search, I applied for several assistant principal and coordinator positions but received only a few preliminary phone screenings. I saw a job posting online for an assistant superintendent for special services in a neighboring elementary school district. The job description looked similar to the assistant principal for student services position I was applying for at the high school level, so I figured transitioning to an elementary school district central office position would be comparable. (I was wrong.) I applied for the job and was invited to an in-person interview. When I arrived at the interview, I was surprised and unprepared for a one-on-one interview with the superintendent, Dr. Eva Smith. I can still remember the interview to this day.

Typically, I consider myself a good interviewee and feel I am able to read the energy in the room after my responses. But this time, that was not the case. Dr. Smith was stoic, with no affect, no expression at all. She definitely had me rethinking my skill set, and the wind was definitely out of my sails when I left the interview. I knew I had bombed it.

When I got home, I told my wife that it'd been the worst interview of my life—there was no chance I was getting a callback. To my surprise, the superintendent contacted me a couple of days later. She asked me to come in for a second interview with the administrative team. After that second interview, I knew there was no way I was going to get the job. Once again, I was surprised to receive a callback, and even more surprised to get a job offer. To this day, I am thankful for Dr. Smith, who opened the door to my first central office administrative job. She saw something in me I hadn't seen within myself. She passed away a couple of years ago. When she left this earth, I felt like a piece of me left with her. Moving forward, I always wanted to make her proud.

At thirty-four years old, I became the youngest assistant superintendent in the state, and the only male African American assistant superintendent within my age demographic. As with the others' stories of inspirational colleagues shared in this book, I acknowledge how Dr. Smith's legacy lives on within the work I do to this day.

We Often Bend until We Break

You may look at my professional work history, my climb to the role of an assistant superintendent at age thirty-four, and believe I have had a successful career. In some respects, I have. But trust me when I say I've experienced consequences: sacrifices, burnout, and compassion fatigue. Secondary traumatic stress is real.

I didn't have a balance in my life between work and family. I looked at things as either/or. I rationalized overworking by concluding I was supporting my family. I struggled with setting and adhering to my personal boundaries. I had a difficult time saying no. I often allowed myself to be guilted into doing things, or I took on more responsibility at work by starting clubs, groups, and programs. They were needed, and nobody else wanted to handle them. Again, does this sound like a familiar story in the world of education?

My biggest challenge was not taking a break, time for myself, or time for my family. There had been a time I set aside just for me, when we went on vacation every year, but that stopped. I rarely took sick or vacation days, which in some regard came to be beneficial when I needed that time. However, I wouldn't have needed so much sick and vacation time had I been taking time for myself when necessary.

But I'd been too busy chasing the success I perceived others to have while believing I did not measure up. During my darkest hour, the manifestations of my imposter syndrome and my martyrdom finally came to a head with my own substance abuse. The coping mechanisms I had been using to compensate were not only unhealthy but also unsustainable. I had gotten to a point where I could no longer "fake it to make it."

I had to learn the hard way that it's OK to say no; it's OK not to take on everything for everyone.

Today, I am sober, my mental illness is stable, and I am definitely in a better place and space than I was before. I want to offer hope, inspiration, and encouragement through the things I have learned through my personal journey. I want to let you know that if I—a trauma survivor and recovering addict with mental illnesses, suicidal ideation, and a disability (ADHD)—can learn to thrive instead of survive, you can, too.

My message is my story is a cautionary tale for educators not only at the beginning of their careers but at any point. It is a tale of what *not* to do. If you find yourself in a situation like mine, know that things can and will get better.

Practicing self-care and prioritizing yourself will help you be your best for those you serve. And it will enable you to not just survive but also thrive in times of uncertainty and challenge.

Our Perception of the Profession Must Change

If 2020 has taught us anything, it's that we need to take charge of our own personal well-being.

We must change the narrative of martyrdom within our profession. As educators, we are compassionate, empathetic, givers, and fixers by nature. We sometimes care more about those we serve than we care about ourselves. We often lose balance, seldom adhere to our personal boundaries, and feel guilty about taking a break. This is the secret seldom spoken aloud within the education profession but practiced quite often among our peers. We must continuously remind ourselves and believe that the number one advocate for you is you.

We need to allow ourselves permission to prioritize ourselves and be SELFish about our self-care and personal wellness in order to be SELFless for others we serve.

The overall goal isn't to change your lifestyle overnight but, through the power of self-awareness and self-reflection, to implement small changes in your lifestyle that may lead to personal and professional transformation.

To make the same impact on others that educators like Dr. Smith made on me, I have to first ensure that I make a positive impact on myself. We have to know that we have to take care of ourselves, because, at the end of the day, that is all we have. Our legacy will never live on in others if we don't nurture it in ourselves.

Three Questions for Conversation

1. What are some things you do to practice self-care outside of the classroom?
2. One of the hardest things for an educator to say is "no," but we can't be all things to all people. What advice would you give to others for saying "no" without feeling guilty or as if they haven't done enough?
3. When you have been at a place where you have felt overwhelmed in your work/learning, what things have you done to find more balance so that you can take better care of yourself?

MORE ABOUT EVAN WHITEHEAD

Evan Whitehead has been an educator for more than twenty years. His career has spanned three decades in private, public, and state-level education. He has held positions ranging from special education paraprofessional and teacher to assistant superintendent. Most recently, Evan was named one of the top fifty culture builders of 2020 by *Award Winning Culture*. Evan is also a national consultant, trainer, and presenter with Dr. Ruby K. Payne's Aha! Process (ahaprocess.com), a speaker, frequent podcast contributor, mental health advocate, mindfulness practitioner, and advocate of equity, diversity, and intercultural competency. Evan's "Three Bs"—balance, boundaries, and breaks (aka #BalanceBoundariesandBreaks)—promote a lifestyle of self-advocacy in the areas of mental health, mindset, self-care, and well-being. Currently, Evan is the director of special services for a PK–8 school district in Illinois. In his current role, he oversees special education, English learners, early childhood education, multi-tiered system of supports, and social-emotional learning, equity, diversity, and cultural competency. You can connect with Evan on Twitter at @evanwhitehead00.

16

Connections Are Cornerstones to Our Hearts

LAUREN KAUFMAN

Everything you want in life is a relationship away.
—Idowu Koyenikan

We've all experienced significant moments in time that have transformed our perspectives and altered the paths we walked. These significant moments often engender a multitude of feelings and encourage us to make choices that impact the direction of our lives. These moments can be difficult to see in real time because we become so consumed with the experience itself.

These are the moments that unlock our potential, help us stand in our power, and ensure we continually evolve. Very often these moments are revealed through new experiences and with the various people we encounter throughout our lives. Whether we perceive these interactions as productive or unfavorable, they empower us to reflect on who we are and who we want to be, and they expose our true purpose in life.

Rewinding Time

When I think back to my first year of teaching, I can't help but wish I could conveniently press the rewind button and replay the pivotal moments that changed the course of my educational journey. I love the thought of going back in time, and if I were afforded the opportunity, I'd give my younger self the most heartfelt and meaningful (yet practical) advice.

I'd walk right alongside that first-year teacher, providing the encouragement that would have my younger self immediately embracing insight earned over the course of almost two decades: keep kids at the heart of decision-making at all times. Relationships and connections are the epicenters of everything you do. Take risks, and try new and better practices. Trust your instincts. Seek out professional development because you absolutely shouldn't wait for it to come to you. Take all of the educators you have ever admired and be the best version of them. Find a community of support. Give yourself grace and certainly take a break!

"One more important thing," I'd tell her because this particular tip would come in handy sooner than she knew. "Do yourself a favor and learn how to administer the Heimlich maneuver."

Yes, I administered it within my first years of teaching. Crazy, right? All of the things I just mentioned are extremely important, and I felt an obligation to share them, especially because in my current role, it is my responsibility to mentor new teachers and help them build a strong foundation that will set them on paths to long, meaningful careers.

Although everything I acknowledged above is sound, valuable advice, I am really here to share a story. From the moment we start teaching, the stories we create live in the memory boxes of our minds, waiting to be courageously unwrapped and gifted to people who can use them to discover ideas and recognize their own passions. In an *Innovator's Mindset* podcast, George Couros brilliantly says, "Stories are the fuel for innovation. They inspire us. They give us pertinent ideas. They get the work we are doing out to people in a really compelling way that goes beyond what a score could tell people about our students."

Beneath the facade of every human being lies personal, unique collections of stories that reveal reflections of who they are and who they want to be. How can we intentionally create spaces for new teachers to reflect on how they are impacting their learners and share how they view the world through stories?

The Interview of a Lifetime

The moment that launched my first year of teaching still lives and thrives in my memory. I mean, how could I possibly forget the interview of a lifetime that provided me the opportunity to have a classroom of my own? Even now, I can conjure a crisp image in my mind: the heart of a busy urban area, the unfamiliar building, and its faded yellow bricks.

As I stepped out of my car, I heard the sounds of a bustling morning. Buses pulled up to the main entrance, while droves of families dropped off their children to the thud of closing car doors. I can still hear the sounds of those children chattering as they rushed into the building. Nearby teachers informally shared their plans for the day or told stories about their families.

My lungs filled with air as I closed my eyes and took the deepest breath you could possibly imagine. That breath was layered with nervousness and fear, but it was also filled with promise and hope for what could be the beginning of a very important journey. I remember making eye contact with a few teachers who were entering the building at the same time as me. They gave me that look—you know the one. It seemed to say, "Another new young teacher trying to land her first job—take a number!" But it was also the look of empathy and encouragement, if that even makes sense. I mean, every teacher on the planet has been on that first interview. It's never easy. It's never comfortable. It's *always* awkward.

In no time, the security guard was escorting me to the main office, where I locked eyes with the principal and assistant principal for the first time. They were sitting in a dimly lit office around an oval-shaped desk, papers stacked on its surface. My first thought was there were hundreds of cover letters and résumés, all from hopeful educators who they'd been interviewing for a single job. At that moment, a voice inside me said I was in way over my head.

That voice continued to echo in my ear. *Why me?* it taunted. *Do I deserve to be here? Will they see qualities in me that will leave a lasting impression? How could they consider giving someone with such a sparse résumé and only a year's experience as a teaching assistant the opportunity to embark on the most important job in the world, impacting the lives of children?*

My erratic internal thinking was interrupted by the sound of my name. I found the principal and assistant principal looking at me with inviting smiles. In an enthusiastic tone of voice, the principal said, "Lauren, please come in, sit down, and just make yourself comfortable!" Right then and there, the deep breath of air that had filled my lungs released as quickly as a balloon rapidly deflating.

As soon as I sat down, the principal began firing questions at me. Oh man, I felt like a bull's-eye on a dart board and the darts were pelting me left and right. Before I could fully process one question, I was providing a mediocre, surface-level answer. I could barely catch my breath before it was time to answer the next. And since I barely had any experience to draw from, almost all of my answers to those questions started with, "Well, if I were to have my own classroom, I'd . . ." Not once did I say, "This is who I am as an educator, this is what I do, and let me give examples of how I do it."

To be honest, it felt like I was totally bombing the interview. I didn't have the most practical responses. My answers weren't neatly wrapped and tied with a bow of acronyms, buzzwords, and delightful stories educators use to show they know what they are talking about. I specifically remember catching the principal and assistant principal making eye contact after each of my answers. They'd smirk, nod, and jot down some notes without actually looking at the paper. I asked myself, "Is that a good sign, or is she smiling and agreeing that my amateur answers were totally off and completely unacceptable?"

At the end of the interview Principal Beth Longo paused and said, "Lauren, it's over. You can breathe now. Are you OK?" Embarrassment pushed on my heart, and my cheeks felt like they were on fire. I couldn't see them, but I knew they were bright red, as if I had just run a novice interview marathon. But my goodness, it was over! I was still sitting there alive and well (and, yes, I was breathing). Hey, I lived to tell this story, didn't I?

And then the final question arrived. "Lauren, do you know why you are here?"

No, I really didn't. But I ventured a guess. "Ummm," I said innocently, "did you like my résumé?" I probably looked just as confused as I felt. I thought back to the fifty hard-copy résumés I had mailed to various schools within three out of five New York City boroughs. It was still hard to believe that I received only two phone calls for interviews. I tried to remember if this school had any particular significance during that adventure.

"Actually, I noticed on the very bottom of your résumé you included that you worked for the same cosmetics company my daughter still works for," Beth said.

My mind was instantly trying to process what she was saying while flipping through a mental filing cabinet of names in a desperate attempt to connect her last name with anyone I had crossed paths with in the eight years, about twenty stores, and five states I had worked in the cosmetics industry. But amid all that mental shuffling, I gave myself a pat on the back for reluctantly including that information on my résumé. After all, the experience did not relate to education. I had to come out and just ask, "Who is your daughter, Ms. Longo?"

"Erica," she said. "You worked with her at Saks Fifth Avenue in New York City. And don't worry. She is the best reference you could possibly ask for because she will tell me the truth!"

"Of course, I remember your daughter. Wait, Erica is *your* daughter?" Did I miss something here? I stood by the Saks cosmetics counter with Erica for years. I mean, we hadn't been close friends, but when the store was slow, we talked about everything under the sun: our friends, our families, our fun stories about living our best lives in our twenties. But how had I missed that her mom was a veteran principal?

"I called her right away, before I called you in for this interview. Do you want to know what she told me about you, Lauren? She told me that you are responsible. You are dedicated. You are an outstanding communicator. You are sincere and passionate. You are curious. You are a learner who seeks growth. She told me that you set goals and will take actionable steps to persevere, achieve them, and then set new ones. That's the type of person I want to work with in my building. That's the type of model I want the kids and my faculty to see. These are the skills you need to be a team player and be successful if you plan to have a long career in education. Because you know what? This work is hard. This work is emotional, and there are times it will be incredibly draining. But it's rewarding, Lauren, it really is! So what if your answers about content, curriculum, instruction, and lesson planning were average at best? You will learn all of that on the front lines. But do you know what's harder to learn? Interpersonal skills, commitment, dedication, and a desire to build strong connections, maintain a positive spirit, and possess the willingness to grow. According to what I saw today and from what my daughter shared, you *are* those things. So, I have ten more interviews today, but if I call you tonight and offer you the job, will you accept?"

I didn't wait too long to answer. With a bright, wide-eyed, cheesy, new-teacher grin, I said, "Of course. Yes, yes I will!"

Putting in the Work

In the two years I was fortunate enough to be in that school, I invested time in learning about my colleagues and students. I implemented a rigorous curriculum and became a master at changing my fancy bulletin boards by the first of every month. This included making sure that all student work was published to perfection, learning targets were prominently displayed, performance tasks were clear, and student feedback was displayed with appropriate glow and grow comments. No wonder I was hospitalized for a kidney infection during my first year of teaching. I never allowed myself time to even go to the bathroom. I mean, who has time to go to the bathroom in their first year of teaching when there is so much to do?

The work seemed never-ending. Looking back, I think I created more work for myself than necessary. Obviously, that mindset needed to change. I mean, who has time to be glued to a hospital bed for a week in their first year of teaching—or, for that matter, any year of teaching? It should be a requirement for all first-year teachers to be mindful about slowing down, taking a break, and practicing self-care daily.

My classroom was a revolving door. Beth and various administrators from other buildings would visit to not only give me positive feedback but also provide me with constructive advice so I could grow. After my first year of teaching second grade (the grade all newbies started teaching until they could prove that they were capable of teaching a "testing" grade), I learned I would be moving to fifth grade because I was ready to take on the big leagues, so to speak. Looking back, the notion of fifth grade being more important is silly; I know now that every grade level matters. It takes a village, and we all depend on one another to maximize the social-emotional and academic potential within every learner we serve.

I have to admit, I instantly cried nervous tears when I got my new assignment. Wow, how childish and embarrassing! Beth, who was a straight shooter with a big heart, told me to get it together and explained that this was a good move because I would be challenged.

So, I got it together. I got it together so well that I was given a student teacher in my second year of teaching. That's why it was such a surprise when everything went south.

I was called into the office on a hot June day during my second year of teaching. In the same office where I was offered the opportunity of a lifetime, I learned—at nine months pregnant with my first son, no less—that due to budgetary constraints, I would be excessed along with three other incredible teachers. I'd be out of a job in just one month's time.

This decision came down to dollars and cents, and I was assured it had nothing to do with my performance. Still, there I was, crying my eyes out (again). I had experienced all of the emotions one can endure in that small, dimly lit office: laughter, happiness, joy, hope, sadness, and disappointment.

The Team You Start with May Not Be
the Team You Grow with

On Brené Brown's *Dare to Lead* podcast, Simon Sinek mentioned that the team you start with isn't the team you necessarily grow with. He said, "Faith is knowing that you are on a team even if you don't know who the players are."

This idea reflects and reinforces the experiences I have encountered throughout my educational journey. I really thought I would be at that school forever. It felt like home for two years, and for a while after hearing that this school didn't fit into my future, disappointment and sadness suffocated me. It felt like the end of the world.

Best-selling author Nic Stone recently visited my school community and reflected on the endings of her books. "The end is a new beginning," she said. "When you get to the end of the path, you start a new one."

I believe that the universe placed Beth in my life at the right time. She was the one who gave me a foot in the door. She gave me the chance to spread my wings and provided a safe space to learn, thrive, fail, and fly. And when I left the nest, she was always right there when I needed her. She was an incredible reference when I obtained jobs in another New York City school and the Long Island, New York, school district I'm currently working in.

Beth and I kept in touch for thirteen years. She constantly used Facebook to comment on pictures of my growing children and to just check in and say, "Hi, how are you?"

Then one day, I received the most awful phone call. Beth lost her battle to cancer. On that day, my heart crumbled into tiny little pieces. I dropped every commitment I had to attend her funeral. When I entered the funeral home, my gaze soared around the room looking for Beth's daughter Erica. When we finally saw each other, we locked eyes and walked toward each other. Our arms simultaneously opened, and we embraced for a while. "I need to say thank you properly, Erica," I said. "It was because of you that I got my very first job in education. You sent me on the journey of a lifetime, and I am eternally grateful."

"No, Lauren, you got yourself that job by being you," she said. "My mom just saw what I'd always seen in you, and she would be so proud to know what you are doing now. So proud."

What I Know Now

It was then that I realized that no matter where we are in our lives, connections are cornerstones to our hearts and will ultimately be at the core of everything we do. Being intentional with opportunities to connect with others and making sure people feel valued are investments in the work we do every single day.

Very often when we are in the moment, we don't always recognize the connections we are making with others or how we will positively influence their future. I would never have imagined that my career in cosmetics would open the door to an opportunity in education. Never burn your bridges, never underestimate the power of relationships, and always have faith in yourself. This will lead you to the people who will eventually become a part of your team and who have the potential to make a tremendous impact on your life.

When you make an effort to intentionally connect with people, you pave the way to hidden pathways of opportunity that can positively impact your future.

Three Questions for Conversation

1. What are some intentional ways you connect with people, show you care, and make them feel valued?
2. How have the connections you have made with people from your past impacted the kind of educator you are today?
3. How will you use what you have learned from your experiences to increase your impact and expand your influence on the educators you encounter throughout your career?

MORE ABOUT LAUREN KAUFMAN

Lauren Kaufman is an educator whose professional passion is empowering teachers to lead, share their gifts with others, and develop lifelong literacy practices in all learners. In her more than fifteen years in education, she has worked as an elementary classroom teacher, literacy specialist, instructional coach, and creativity camp supervisor. She is currently a middle school literacy specialist and mentor coordinator for K–12 in Long Island, New York. Lauren has led teams in developing seventy-three units of study in reading and writing for K–5, has provided educators with job-embedded professional learning, and guides new teachers in acclimating to the culture and climate of a school system. She continually shares her passion for learning by speaking at conferences, serving on the #EdCampLI planning team, writing blogs and chapters in educational books, and cohosting the #Empathetic_Educators live podcast. You can connect with Lauren on Twitter at @Lau7210, on Instagram at @laurenmkaufman, and through her website, laurenmkaufman.com.

17

The Real Work Is the Work We Do on Ourselves

MEGHAN LAWSON

Life isn't a matter of milestones, but of moments.
—Rose Kennedy

I believe in the power of self-work. It is messy and nonlinear and never-ending. And it's worth it.

I wish I had started working on myself at the beginning of my career—and not just for my sake. My students deserved more than I was able to give them as a new educator. Oh sure, I put in the work. A lot of work. But it turns out, the real work is the work we do on ourselves. Everything else is secondary.

We Don't Have to Be Perfect to Make a Difference

I'm a recovering perfectionist. As a classically trained dancer and Enneagram type three (more about that in a moment), I have a deeply rooted history of perfectionism.

In ballet, I learned the value of practice. It's what made it possible for me to control every movement and polish my body placement. I learned to care about and agonize over all of the little details. At times, this detail-orientation serves me well. It helps me ensure the centerpieces on the tables at professional learning events are just right. It prompts me to craft a killer event playlist. And it makes people feel special and cared for.

Unfortunately, this attention to detail feeds into my perfectionism. Worse, my focus on making myself and my professional moves perfect can reach unhealthy levels when unchecked.

The Enneagram is one of the oldest personality tests. There are nine types, and while the test can't tell you everything there is to know about yourself—personality is complex, after all—it is a helpful framework for self-understanding. I am an Enneagram type three, classified as the achiever. I wish I would have known that sooner because the more I read about type threes, the better I understand myself and my motives.

When Enneagram type threes aren't doing their inner work, they can slip into habits like trying to prove their worth by achieving goals. Sadly, many people have a deep-seated belief that they are not worthy of love and belonging.

I'm sitting here writing this the day after Valentine's Day. We buried my dad on February 14 when I was six years old. Sometimes, on this day of love, people will reach out to remind me how proud my dad would be of the person I've become. I get choked up. I can talk about my dad and about his death without crying fairly easily now, but hearing that he would be proud gets me every time. It's all I ever wanted. To make him proud. To feel and know that he loves me.

But the lesson I'm learning about all relationships—both inside and outside of the classroom—is that we are lovable, and people can be proud of us even when we make mistakes. Even when we aren't perfect. Letting go of perfectionism is one of the greatest gifts I've ever given myself. I've enjoyed many conversations with George Couros, and our conversation about perfection remains one of my favorites. I remember being floored when he told me he was going to quote me in his book *Innovate Inside the Box*. I had told him, "We don't need to be perfect to make a difference. We need to care deeply about our impact on kids, care deeply about our words, and we need to embrace our humanness."

Embracing my humanity has done a lot for me, my relationships, and my work. I can't help but wonder: If Taylor Swift had let a crippling fear of failure get in her way, would she have released not one but two albums within one year? My money's on no. Nothing stifles productivity quite like perfection.

I remind myself of that fact all the time. I don't need to be perfect. That is not my job as a human. My job is to keep going. To keep trying. To keep making mistakes and learning and loving myself through that process. And all the while, I'll love others through their faults and foibles.

When I was in a central office role, I was making some big changes in a community that valued tradition. These were changes that I believed were truly good for kids. They were also the kinds of changes that had the potential to blow up in my face—the kinds of changes that lead to angry mobs showing up at board meetings. I envisioned myself torn to shreds on the local news and subsequently losing my job. I was hung up on controlling my every move to keep myself out of the fray. But the obsession with executing my work perfectly was tearing me up on the inside.

Luckily, I had hired a job coach. It may not have been the reason I reached out to her—I was genuinely interested in growing and setting some goals for the future—but this big work gave us great content to sort through during our time together. After listening to me spiral through all of my anxiety over the situation, she said something I will never forget: "Meghan, people don't like perfect people."

What?

Her comment snapped me out of my funk. She was right. When it comes to vulnerability, leaders go first. When we make leadership something only perfect people do, we make everyone in our organization feel like leadership is out of their reach. Then we wonder why teachers or students don't see themselves as leaders.

Leaders have an obligation to practice being human in front of other people. We have an obligation as teachers and administrators to be transparent in our mistakes and learn from them in front of others. In doing so, we make it safe for others to take risks, learn from their mistakes, and talk about it in front of others. When we normalize imperfection, caring deeply, being human, and learning, we start a chain reaction that empowers others to do the same.

Ask yourself: Are you about making an impact or looking shiny? Because it turns out, when we are focused on our impact, our light shines bright and draws others to us.

In my early years as a teacher, I struggled with many common issues. I struggled when I received an angry parent email and took it personally when a student misbehaved in my class. I agonized over my observations. Over the course of my self-work, I realized that worrying about failure and striving for an impossible ideal weren't harming just me; they were harming my ability to help others, too.

When we are in a state of fear and see situations as win or lose, and when we focus on trying to be perfect in those situations, we can't show up the way we need to for others. We can't be deeply curious. We can't be honest about how we're feeling, the mistakes we've made, and what we're learning.

Perfection is the enemy of true connection, belonging, and creativity. And the world needs all of that, perhaps now more than ever.

Everyone is doing the best they can. Including you. Cut yourself some slack.

Just because you don't see yourself in the teaching models that you've been presented with doesn't mean you shouldn't be a teacher or can't be your own version of a great teacher.

For the first four years of my teaching career, I was very impressionable. Instead of focusing on what good teaching looked like and felt like to me, I focused on what good teaching looked like to the veteran teachers in my high school English department. I would take their materials, their lessons, their philosophies on writing instruction, and I would plop them right into my classroom. I would mechanically work through the lessons and grade the papers in a way that I thought would impress them. This focus on other teachers instead of my students did not serve me or my students well. I felt like a robot. I was going through the motions without thinking critically about my students or connecting with my heart.

The uninspired start to my career made me feel like I was an imposter. So, I fell back on what I had read about being a good teacher. I didn't worry about whether I thought the advice was any good because I didn't trust that I had any personal magic to add to the work. I had stuffed my gut instincts into a locked box. Instead of asking whether giving students additional time on an assignment would help them learn or what the impact of giving zeros for homework might be, I relied on the class policies and procedures I had taken from experienced teachers in the building. Surely, they knew more than me; they had been at this a lot longer.

I feel icky on the inside as I recall a memory of getting into a battle with a couple of boys over whether their papers were plagiarized. Students submitted their papers to turnitin.com, and these two were flagged as being overwhelmingly similar, each with a large amount of content from the internet.

To start, I poorly managed this situation by emailing their parents. Here's a tip—if you need to have a very difficult conversation, do it in person or over the phone. Do not send an email. No matter how good with words you think you are, nothing beats the sound of a human voice. Calling or asking for an in-person meeting sends a strong message of care.

These parents got very upset and went to the principal, who I had not told about the situation. That's another tip. If you find yourself in a difficult situation, be sure to talk with leadership about it. Often, those above you will have great advice and insight that will be useful when you take action. Even if you don't get guidance, leadership will show up in a better way for you and for others if they have a heads-up and have time to sort through it.

As important as those revelations were, neither was my big aha moment. I am ashamed to say that not once—not once!—in that entire situation did I reflect upon myself as a teacher and what may have contributed to the approach these boys had taken to their papers. Did I not equip them with the skills they needed to write a paper on their own? Was it boring that I had asked all kids to write to the same prompt on the same book? Would it have helped if they had more choices in their reading and writing? When modeling and scaffolding the writing process, did I inadvertently send the message that it was OK to collaborate on papers that were submitted for individual credit? And *was* it OK? Did this paper matter less because it didn't have an authentic audience? And perhaps the most painful wondering: Had I created a culture in my classroom in which kids didn't feel safe coming to me for help, so they had resorted to cheating?

A couple of years ago, I posted on Twitter about how I had forgotten to bring a writing utensil to a meeting, so someone simply handed me a pen. The comment launched a good old "give the kid a pencil" debate. You know the situation—a kid comes to class without a writing utensil and asks for a pencil.

Many teachers agreed that they'd loan out the pencil, while others argued that they couldn't afford to keep providing pencils to kids. Some suggested we trade students for something they care about. Others said, "Just walk the hallway and your classroom at the end of the day. There are plenty on the floor—no need to purchase them."

Some teachers argued that we needed to "teach these kids responsibility." Another said, "Many kids have more going on in their personal lives than some of us have ever experienced. Some didn't have breakfast and don't have clean clothes to wear to school, so your lesson on school supplies and responsibility is the least of their concerns right now."

And that's closer to where I fall. Now. But I didn't always feel this way about pencils and late homework and do-overs on papers. I've come to realize that there is a lot that I don't control and can't control, but what I can control is how I show up for myself and others and how I learn from what I experience. I would rather remove barriers for kids than make their day more difficult. I would rather help students reach my high expectations for learning than focus on school supplies. And if that means other people think I'm too "soft on crime," so be it. I didn't become a teacher to police the little things. I've learned to care more about my impact on students and my belief in what I'm doing than what people with different values think about my teaching methods.

I'm still learning to look inward. Recently, I was leading a professional learning session, and a few teachers were sending things to the printer while I was presenting. The printer was right by me. It was very obvious what was going on. Now, my first thought was, *Grrr, how rude! Teachers are sometimes the worst students!* But then I started to think about their actions as feedback. By printing during my presentation, they were telling me that they needed more time to plan, that this time of day wasn't good for their learning, that my session wasn't meeting their real needs, or that the presentation wasn't compelling enough at that moment.

None of this makes me a bad presenter. It makes me human. And the information I gathered from the situation brought me one step closer to meeting their needs in the future. What's ironic about this story is that I was filling in for someone who I admire. It was my first time with this group, and I was trying to do things like her! You see, sometimes we have to learn and relearn lessons over and over in our lives. And that's OK. It doesn't mean we are going backward. It means it's an important lesson. So, learn and keep going. But do it your way.

There is only one imperfect you, and that is special. Own that.

I worry sometimes that people pick up education books and think they have to apply all of the lessons all at once—and do it all the same way the author did it. That's overwhelming and discouraging. I've been there and done that. Often, I didn't even realize I was doing it. I used to think that because someone wrote a book, they knew more than I did. After all, I hadn't written a book. Or I would find an educator on social media with a lot more followers than me and assume they knew more than me. *I should really try to do what they say,* I'd tell myself.

This is a dangerous practice! There are a lot of reasons why people have written books or amassed a following, but those "badges of honor" don't guarantee that all of what they say is right or right for you. It also doesn't mean that your ideas or your work is any less important.

What the world needs is more educators who realize how deeply they matter in the lives of others. As Morgan Harper Nichols has said, "You are not any less important than the people you look up to."

Don't forget that. And please don't be afraid to talk about and share your good work with others. Many of the people you look up to are people just like you who have spent a longer time learning in front of others.

Your Happiness Matters in a Big Way

Have you ever found yourself swept up in a show about a topic you don't really care about and yet you're captivated? I recently enjoyed the show *Blown Away* on Netflix, a Canadian reality TV show about a glassblowing competition. I marveled at the art and craft, but most of all I was blown away (pun intended) by the contestants' passion. I was hooked. I binged the entire series and was disappointed when it ended. I now know a lot more about glassblowing and have a new-found appreciation for it. I loved watching their sweat, their hustle, and most of all, their love for their work.

This reminds me of some of the most incredible teachers and leaders from whom I've had the pleasure to learn. We've all had teachers who genuinely enjoyed our company and got excited about the experiences they were creating. That kind of energy sparks positivity and makes the rest of us want to join in the fun and learn, too. These peak moments of connection can be created inside and outside of the classroom.

When we are excited about what we are doing, other people will be excited, too. Emotions are quite literally contagious. We may have something called mirror neurons to thank for that. Scientists are only just beginning to understand how these neurons in our brain play a role in empathy. Just as we might take on the emotions of others—tearing up when someone else cries, for instance—so, too, can other people take on our emotions. So, caring for our mental well-being matters. Planning moments that thrill and delight us matters. This is a form of self-care, and it is not selfish. It is a community act.

When we are happy, a chemical cocktail of dopamine flows through our body, and dopamine has the power to turn on all of the learning centers of our brains. As Shawn Achor has explained, "Our brain at positive is 31 percent more productive than at negative, neutral, or stressed." That is a large percentage! Imagine if you got 31 percent more done in a day. If you had 31 percent more money. If you got 31 percent more sleep. Thirty-one percent is no joke, and yet we don't spend much time focused on this brain research and what happiness can do to help people reach their greatest potential in our schools.

Our students are watching us. They look at us and wonder whether they want to aspire to be educators like us. I wish I would have realized this sooner. I wish I would have understood sooner the deep, moral imperative I have to show kids that this work can be fun. A great way to advance the future of our profession is to make it look like an enjoyable and meaningful one.

This doesn't have to require a lot of planning on our part. What it requires, though, is a willingness to put ourselves out there. As Elizabeth Gilbert says, "Be the weirdo who dares to enjoy."

Enjoyment isn't goofing off. It engages the brain. As it turns out, the brain gets more out of happy, unexpected moments than those that are totally expected. How might we bring more unexpected thrill and delight into the school experience? This can happen inside the classroom but also during those regular, mundane moments of the school day, as well.

I remember inside recess last school year. If you've ever worked in an elementary school, you can appreciate how stressful inside recess can get. Many students need the opportunity to run around and let out energy, and sometimes a puzzle just doesn't cut it. So, when we could, we brought the students into the gym.

Now, bringing kids into the gym has its own challenges. Without zones for the activities, it can get wild. I giggle as I write that and picture the scene from *Kindergarten Cop* in which Arnold Schwarzenegger's character has lost all control of the classroom. In an effort to promote a sense of play that also felt safe, we had to get creative.

Whatever was in my brain as silly and fun, I just went for it. I can distinctly remember a day at second-grade recess when I started a conga line. So, there I was, by myself in the middle of the wild, stepping and rolling my arms and throwing a pointed finger to the side. Many kids stopped what they were doing to look. Their faces said it all. "What is our principal doing? That looks funny . . . and fun. I might want to join . . ."

It started with a couple of kiddos getting behind me in the line. And then a few more. And more. And more. Before I knew it, I had a majority of the second grade behind me. Laughing and adding their own fun, personal flair to the conga. As I laughed and looked behind me at this performance, I caught the eye of the two second-grade teachers who were monitoring recess. They had their phones out, taking pictures, smiling, and seemingly relieved that, for even just a moment, they could catch their breath.

So often we think of keeping order and safety in school as being centered on rules and expectations. Sure, there are certain things that must be in place. But a third-grade student said it best when he told me, "Want to know why I'm doing good in school? It's not because of the rules. It's because you're my best friend."

A great way to build those best friendships is through fun and play. These are peak moments of connection. When I was playing dragons at recess with my third-grade friend, I would stop, breath my "fire," and watch what he would do next. In those free play moments, I marveled at his creativity and ability to improvise and think sharply on his feet—things that I probably wouldn't see on his reading test. There are hidden jewels inside of children, and our job as educators is to find them.

I'm drawn to TV shows like *Zoey's Extraordinary Playlist*, in which characters break out into song seemingly out of nowhere. In those performances (that only Zoey can see and hear), she experiences a deeper level of connection to their true selves and underlying emotions.

When we create enthusiasm and happiness around others, we inspire them to enjoy in very authentic ways. And we get to experience who they are on a deeper level as a result.

We can all do it in a way that feels honest and true to who we are as human beings and professionals. This is not separate from the work. It's critical to our work. As Chip and Dan Heath warn in *The Power of Moments*, "Beware of the soul-sucking force of reasonableness."

Let's dare to enjoy. In doing so, we invite others to do the same, and the happiness we create for others gives them greater access to their big potential.

How people feel is just as important as what people learn.

So, I leave you with this—you matter. Your work matters. Your words matter. What you do and say in your classroom every day matters. As Peter Block says, "How do you change the world? One room at a time. Which room? The one you're in."

Keep showing up. We need you.

Three Questions for Conversation

1. Who are some people you can ask for critical feedback often? Getting comfortable with imperfections and critical feedback is a superpower.

2. Which professional voices do you respect? How can you respect those voices while honoring your teacher's gut even more? Remember, you know things. Your voice is no less valuable.

3. How might you bring thrills and delight into your daily life and into the lives of students? Happiness matters in a big way.

MORE ABOUT MEGHAN LAWSON

Meghan is a thought leader who studies and implements the conditions and systems needed for transformational change. A lover of learning who believes in the goodness of people, Meghan works to cultivate safe spaces that honor the humanity of all people. She promotes storytelling, the exchange of ideas, and risk-taking. She is passionate about disrupting the status quo and creating kinder, more forward-thinking communities of action. Meghan is also intensely curious about how to enhance the customer experience in schools. She began her career in the English Language Arts classroom. So, inevitably, her mantra is "words matter." In her more than seventeen years in the field, she has worked in all levels of K–12 education as a teacher, school administrator, district administrator, and educational consultant. You can connect with Meghan on Twitter at @meghan_lawson, on Instagram at @meghanlawsonblog, or on her blog at meghanlawson.com.

Moving Forward:

I Will Cherish the Impact You Have Had on My Life Forever

GEORGE COUROS

Children are likely to live up to what
you believe of them.
—Lady Bird Johnson

I remember seeing a video hosted by SoulPancake (of Kid President fame) that brought tears of pride and joy to my eyes.

The video was a tribute to a teacher named Mrs. Flexer, who after forty-one years of teaching had decided to retire. To honor her, many of her former students came together to surprise her and share the incredible impact she had on their lives.

The video scans a crowded classroom full of former students before it snags on a cracked-open door. From somewhere down the hall, Mrs. Flexer closes in. In the brief moment before she enters the space, another teacher approaches to guide her inside. If you listen closely, you can hear Mrs. Flexer say, "Everything good?"

That might seem like an insignificant moment, but the two words remind me of the care so many teachers have for their children. Even in those few-and-far-between moments when teachers are recognized for the incredible impact they have on the lives of others, they're more concerned for the safety and well-being of the kids in their care. To outsiders, her question might have seemed insignificant, but to anyone who has taught, it was the norm.

She enters the classroom to raucous applause, her jaw dropping at the sight of her former students. She is clearly overwhelmed with emotion as she takes in every person in that space, and I can only imagine she has some recollection of their time in her care. Students don't just get a teacher for a year. They often end up with a lifelong cheerleader and advocate, as I did with Mrs. Stock, my kindergarten teacher, who is probably reading this book.

As the video continues, former students share stories and heartfelt memories of Mrs. Flexer. In one of my favorite moments, a young woman talks about how Mrs. Flexer heard her sing a song in class and was so proud that she asked the young student to go from class to class, serenading other students. Mrs. Flexer's belief in her abilities helped her believe in herself, and that lasted long into adulthood.

As I relisten to the stories in this video, overcome by emotion (the video has 3.4 million views as of writing this, and I think about three million of those are from me), there is a line from a former student that, to me, summarizes everything education should be, "You hold such a special place in my heart, and I will cherish the impact you have had on my life forever."

Excuse me while I pause the video to stop crying.

Those words. That sentence. That is everything a teacher aspires to be, and everything teachers become to so many people—whether they know it or not.

The stories from Mrs. Flexer's former students all speak of one teacher's extraordinary belief in her students and the inspiring actions and words that have contributed to who they became.

But it is also important to note what is *not* shared. Not one of the students mentions any exam or even specific content. They all mention connection.

I have said this forever and believe it to this day: if we teach children only the curriculum, we have failed them. Mrs. Flexer taught the kids hope, self-belief, and love. The curriculum might have been forgotten over time, but those lessons remained.

Your Impact

Every time I see this video, I wish that every teacher would have the same experience. I wish that at the end of their career they'd find a room full of former students and their families. I wish they'd hear an oral history of the impact they had on the lives of their students and get a reminder of the legacy they created in their classrooms.

A teacher's influence doesn't stay in school. It goes out into the world and cannot truly ever be measured. Every student you inspire to do something great goes on to inspire others. There is no limit to your impact.

I also know that because of fire codes and other things, only a small sample of Mrs. Flexer's students were able to attend her retirement party. She no doubt affected the lives of more students than we can count in that video. In all likelihood, she impacted more students than she taught in her four-decade career. As educators, our impact has the potential to span the entire school. We often touch the lives of students we never teach—those we see in the hallways, connect with at recess, and encounter at numerous community events. With seemingly simple gestures, we can have an impact on kids and never truly know it.

I remember being at a professional learning day led by the incredible Deidre Roemer, who shared an amazing story earlier in this book about her father and his impact as an educator. I see his story in her. She had brought students together to share their experiences in school with a group of administrators, not only to highlight the great things happening but also to provide suggestions of how they could make things better.

I remember one student specifically. She shared a story about how she had struggled for years in high school and even contemplated suicide. I will never forget her story or the fact that one of the things that helped her get up each day was seeing a teacher every morning in the hallways at her school. She had never had him as a teacher, but every morning, he would greet her by name and provide a warm acknowledgment. That simple act made her want to get up each day and attend school.

I was in tears listening to her, and was reminded of something I liked to share with my staff as a principal: every time we pass a student or colleague in the hallway, we have the opportunity to make their day better with a simple acknowledgment and greeting, and every time we don't say something, it is an opportunity lost. What may seem like such a little thing to one person can mean everything to someone else.

Her story warmed my heart and made me so proud to be an educator. And it reminded me of something Todd Whitaker said: "The best part about being a teacher is, it matters. The hardest part about being a teacher is, it matters every day."

What You Do Matters More Than You Will Ever Know

In this book, you've encountered stories of great educators who've had a long-lasting impact on their colleagues and students. But they're hardly outliers. There are countless educators who make a difference in the lives of those around them—it is why #BecauseofaTeacher became a book. Like the hashtag, this book aims to share inspiring stories of the past to further inspire the classrooms of the future.

The questions that all of the contributors answered truly matter. Thinking of a teacher who inspired you will remind you of your reasons for becoming an educator in the first place. It can make you think of what you wanted to become as well as how your vision of education was modeled by incredible teachers in your past.

Considering the administrators who inspired you will remind you of how important support is in the journey of an educator. In my opinion, the best administrators do everything they can to support teachers as they make an impact on students, and they know that successful teaching could *never* be measured by a test score, only the effect on children's lives.

Finally, by contemplating the advice you would give to your first-year teacher self, you'll remember that although so many teachers set the bar for what we want education to be, they, like all of us, are on a journey of growth and are continuous learners. No teacher just arrived one day and was "great." Yet every teacher can make an impact from day one. On some of your hardest days, you are still inspiring positive memories that your students will look back on in the future. Never take that for granted.

We Need to Share Our Stories

My hope for this book is that it will remind you why you do what you do. More than that, I hope it inspires you to share the stories of our profession that have made such a positive impact on the world. Tell the world about the educators who left their mark on you when you were just a student. But also spread the word about the people across the hallway who made a difference in your life.

To be honest, we often take for granted the incredible things our community makes happen in our schools because we see them every day. They are our norm, but that doesn't make them any less incredible. Who better to tell the story of education than the people who are in our schools today?

I encourage you to share your stories through a tweet, Instagram post, YouTube video, TikTok post, or any other form of social media, using the hashtag #BecauseofaTeacher. Educators need to become the biggest advocates, not only for our students but also for each other.

But, hey, social media might not be your jam, and that is also cool. So, make a phone call. Write a letter. Send a text. Whatever you need to do to get the word out. Let the educators that have made an impact on your life know that you still cherish them.

Imagine if every person reading this book did that. It wouldn't be a true measure of all of the people who have inspired us in education, but it would be a great start. My personal belief is that it is always better to share gratitude too early rather than too late.

As a former student, a constant learner, a forever educator, and a dad, I just want to say thank you on behalf of myself, the collaborators of this book, and all those who you have inspired. As Mrs. Flexer's former student said in that viral YouTube video, "I will cherish the impact you have had on my life forever."

If no one else tells you that today, then at least you read it here. Come back to this page and these stories as many times as you need to remind yourself of your impact.

Because of a teacher like you, the world is a better place.

Three Questions for Conversation

I will ask you to think about the three questions that were the basis of this book and share them in a way that you see fit.

1. Who is a teacher who inspired you and why?
2. Who is an administrator who inspired you and why?
3. What advice would you give to your first-year teacher self?

Think about them and share them with someone who you think would benefit from hearing your answers!

Acknowledgments

First of all, I want to acknowledge my own teachers from my educational experience. As I shared in the book, they reached out to me after I posted a YouTube video talking about their impact on me, and that inspired me to put this thing together. What a beautiful reminder that, as a teacher, you can still continue to inspire your students long after their time in your classroom.

Thank you to all of the contributors of this book who not only wrote their incredible stories on short notice but did so in a way that brought emotions out in me as I read them that reminded me why I do the work that I do today.

The entire editing team of IMPress has been incredible through this process, and I love how they can turn words into an art form through their creativity and professionalism.

Thank you to my incredible wife, Paige, who is probably the best teacher I have ever met in my life, and then also became the best mom I have ever witnessed. She juggles all of that while leading the entire team to bring this book together, and then I watch everyone marvel at how incredibly gracious and kind she is through the process. I am amazed by all that you do for our family each and every day.

And finally, to my beautiful daughters, Georgia and Kallea. You are the fuel that ignites my passion for living each day. Seeing the world through your eyes brings me joy that I never could have imagined. My life is better because of both of you.

More from

IM PRESS

ImpressBooks.org

Innovate inside the Box
Empowering Learners Through UDL and Innovator's Mindset
by George Couros and Katie Novak

Empower
What Happens when Students Own Their Learning
by A.J. Juliani and John Spencer

Learner-Centered Innovation
Spark Curiosity, Ignite Passion, and Unleash Genius
by Katie Martin

Unleash Talent
Bringing Out the Best in Yourself and the Learners You Serve
by Kara Knollmeyer

Reclaiming Our Calling
Hold On to the Heart, Mind, and Hope of Education
by Brad Gustafson

Take the L.E.A.P.
Ignite a Culture of Innovation
by Elisabeth Bostwick

Drawn to Teach
An Illustrated Guide to Transforming Your Teaching
written by Josh Stumpenhorst and illustrated by Trevor Guthke

Math Recess
Playful Learning in an Age of Disruption
by Sunil Singh and Dr. Christopher Brownell

Personal & Authentic
Designing Learning Experiences That Last a Lifetime
by Thomas C. Murray

Learner-Centered Leadership
A Blueprint for Transformational Change in Learning Communities
by Devin Vodicka

Kids These Days
*A Game Plan for (Re)Connecting with Those We
Teach, Lead, & Love*
by Dr. Jody Carrington

UDL and Blended Learning
Thriving in Flexible Learning Landscapes
by Katie Novak and Catlin Tucker

Teachers These Days
Stories & Strategies for Reconnection
by Dr. Jody Carrington and Laurie McIntosh

CPSIA information can be obtained
at www.ICGtesting.com
Printed in the USA
BVHW051946071021
618390BV00004B/17

9 781948 334334